·The·
POET'S
HAND-
BOOK

Judson Jerome

WRITER'S DIGEST BOOKS

Cincinnati, Ohio

Other fine Writer's Digest Books are available from your local bookstore or direct from the publisher.

02 01 00 99   14 13 12 11

Library of Congress Cataloging-in-Publication Data

Jerome, Judson.
    The poet's handbook.

    Includes indexes.
    1. English language—Versification. 2. Poetry—Authorship. I. Title.
PE 1509.J47   808.1   80-17270
ISBN 0-89879-219-3

Book design by Barron Krody.

Other fine Writer's Digest Books are available from your local bookstore or direct from the publisher. A complete catalog of Writer's Digest Books is available FREE by writing to the address shown below, or by calling toll-free 1-800-289-0963. To order additional copies of this book, send in retail price of the book plus $3.50 postage and handling for one book, and $1.50 for each additional book. Ohio residents add 6% sales tax. Allow 30 days for delivery.

Writer's Digest Books
1507 Dana Avenue
Cincinnati, Ohio 45207

Stock is limited on some titles; prices subject to change without notice.

Write to the above address for information on *Writer's Digest* magazine, *Story* magazine, Writer's Digest School, and Writer's Digest Criticism Service.

For Marty and Sandy

who keep making me think how to explain things

with love

ALSO BY JUDSON JEROME

Light in the West (poems)

The Fell of Dark (novel)

Plays for an Imaginary Theater (verse plays and autobiographical essays)

Culture out of Anarchy: the Reconstruction of American Higher Learning

I Never Saw . . . (poems for children)

Families of Eden: Communes and the New Anarchism

Poetry: Premeditated Art

The Poet and the Poem

Thirty Years of Poetry: Poems 1949-1979

Myrtle Whimple's Sampler

Publishing Poetry

Public Domain

The Village . . .

Partita in Nothing Flat

Acknowledgments

Contents

How to Use This Book

How to Use This Book

Here I have felt free to be unabashedly technical, though I have taken pains to explain even the simplest technical terms, usually more than once. These terms are in **boldface type** when they first occur in a passage where they are explained. The Index to Terms (page 217) lists the terms alphabetically with page references to key passages. For a more scholarly treatment of these and thousands of other terms, consult the *Princeton Encyclopedia of Poetry and Poetics* (Princeton University Press), a reference work of inestimable value to any serious poet. The Index to Poets Quoted (page 221) and Index to Works of Poetry Quoted (page 223) provide further cross-references to illustrative material; and the Versification Chart (page 213) summarizes the key terms in a way that I hope will assist memory.

These features make the book a reference work much like a handbook for engineers or physicians, but it differs from such handbooks in two important ways. First, I have put the technical material into a discursive and, I hope, readable discussion, attempting to explain why the terms are used, why they are important, and how these techniques can be used effectively. Thus it is not only a reference book for those who need information or need to brush up on knowledge already acquired, but an instruction manual for those learning to write poetry. It has astonished me, in the more than four decades that I have been struggling to learn about poetry and how to write it, that no such instruction manual has been available. There are many good books on how to write fiction, nonfiction, greeting cards, and other things, but I have seen none on how to write good modern poetry, the kind of poetry published in quality magazines and literary magazines today.

The reader I had in mind was myself, in my teens, looking for the guidance that would enable me to commit a large portion of my life to learning about and writing poetry. I figured that if I could make this book intelligible to a bright, verbal, interested teenager, it would perforce make sense to older readers as well. This did not require "writing down." It forced me to a reconsideration of fundamentals that has helped me discover principles I had been using for years without a very precise understanding of them. Any teacher will tell you he or she learns, in the process of teaching, more than the students. I have learned much from this book.

The second element, in addition to instruction, that makes this book differ from other technical handbooks is argument. I see no reason to disguise my opinions with a pretense of objectivity. Poetry in the United States is in a deplorable condition. More people are writing poetry than ever before, often without any particular knowledge, study, practice, or understanding of the art, and often without much interest in literature. More poetry is being published than ever before. Literally hundreds of little magazines, subsidized by government, universities, foundations, or patrons, are chewing their way through the forests of Canada, flourishing independently of any reader interest. Hundreds of small presses, with the same subsidies, are bringing out thousands of thin volumes of poetry each year, most of them doomed to be unread. Most of the poetry in these publications is unreadable, unintelligible, dull, blindly self-absorbed, formally aimless, and sloppy. The best one can say for it is that it is expressive. Lots of people are certainly expressing themselves, to no one in particular (or in general). It is too easy to get published. Poetry is apparently easy to write.

Why this outpouring in poetry rather than prose? People aren't even writing letters or keeping journals much anymore. They are turning the tides of their feelings into short blobs of writing which are much less demanding. From the examples they have seen published all around them they have deduced that a poem need have no special point. Rules of punctuation, grammar, sentence structure, coherence, accuracy, and significance are suspended. Anything goes. Poetry legitimates narcissism in this Age of Narcissus. One can become absorbed in one's own image and be indifferent to whether or not there is an audience besides oneself. Who needs a handbook to learn how to do *that*?

About 1949 I took a course in poetry with the poet J. V. Cunningham at the University of Chicago. Cunningham had studied with Ivor Winters, who represented what might be called the right wing of the so-called New Criticism that was then prevalent in literary circles. "If this were a course in elephants," he began, "we would have to know what an elephant is. What is poetry?" For an hour or so he listened to us thrash around with our moonlight-in-a-frog's-belly speculations (to use a phrase of Sandburg's). Then he said that, as far as he was concerned, poetry was metrical writing. If it were anything else besides that, he didn't know what it was. I was infuriated. That sounded like something my family might have said. He was ignoring all the emotive, inspirational, intuitive, mystical, expressive qualities of poetry and reducing the art to mere mechanics. Metrical writing indeed!

But unwillingly I recognized that he had a point. On the one hand, poetry is anything you want to call it. If you say it is poetry, it is poetry, and no one can deny it. That doesn't mean it is good poetry. And most good poetry, whatever its other qualities, is metrical writing.

Metrical means measured. A measure, or predetermined form, forces a poet to put his thoughts into a framework. The framework requires the poet to pick and choose, polish, twist, to manage these contortions with grace. It is the tug-of-war between form and content that makes the art of the poem. Prose lies flat on the page. Poetry (good poetry, that is) stands up off it, rounded like a piece of sculpture, because of its imposed form.

That is a recognition that **poetry** is usually **verse.** The two words are generally used (in this book and elsewhere) interchangeably. Technically, however, *poetry* refers to content; *verse,* to form. If you look up the etymology of the two terms you find that *poetry* means "made up," a Greek word for the same idea as "fiction," which has a Latin root. *Verse* means a "turning," a reference to the formal characteristic that it is written in lines. Lines of prose (as the etymology of the word implies) go right on to and past the margin. They are not units of composition. Lines of verse might be longer than a page can accommodate on one line (as are many of the lines of Whitman), but they are usually shorter, giving the poem a visual pattern on the page. How long should the lines be? Usually they adhere to some measure, some length based upon an arbitrary, external, formal factor, such as the number of stresses, of syllables, or of the combination of stresses and syllables we recognize as accentual syllabic feet. Putting writing into measures of this sort is called *versification*. The way we distinguish between other kinds of "made up" writing and poetry is by recognizing versification. We can tell that piece of writing was meant as a poem by the way it looks on the page.

These may seem, as Professor Cunningham's definition of poetry seemed to me, mechanical distinctions. But we have to start there, with the objective differences between poetry and prose. In this book I return again and again to the fundamental question: Why are the lines divided as they are? What is the measure? That is the question I never found adequately dealt with in my own education as a poet.

Another basic question (one which I believe poets too rarely ask themselves) is, What is this writing *for*? I have mentioned one purpose: expression. Many write poetry to get things off their chests. It makes them feel better. But as therapy, poetry is the business of medicine, not of art. I am concerned with poetry as an art form. To some extent this may mean no more than tasteful arrangement of words, images, rhythms, and other characteristics of language. Poetry can be like much music, painting, and sculpture: an abstract pattern, not intended to *mean* anything, but to be somehow beautiful or otherwise aesthetically pleasing in itself. ("Pleasing" may not mean "pleasant." A horror story, or material which is shocking or disturbing or ugly, can be aesthetically pleasing; that is, it may satisfy some kind of aesthetic need or evoke an emotional response which one desires, even though it be a painful experience.) The poet needs the skill to evoke such a response, to manipulate the feelings of an audience, and (as I hope the book demonstrates) the techniques of poetic form can be used more or less well for such purposes.

But most readers, including myself, want more of poetry. In addition to its musical, rhythmical, colorful, emotional, and other characteristics, language has a primary function in human affairs of conveying meaning. Artists of all sorts, including poets, may be satisfied with compositions which have strong aesthetic effects but mean nothing in particular. Readers, though, generally want to *understand* what they read. They think of language primarily in terms of meaning. They want it to make sense. Sense is what keeps them interested, draws them along. The other aesthetic characteristics of language work on their subconscious responses. They may not *know* that they like and remember certain passages of poetry because of their rhythm or sound combinations or other characteristics. They *think* they like poetry for what it says.

It seems to me that a good poet should understand this, should want to lure readers into his or her art, and should therefore be as concerned about having a good sturdy thread of comprehensible meaning running through the work as an engineer should be concerned that a bridge stand up and bear traffic, regardless of how beautiful the bridge may be. Readers can enjoy nonsense such as " 'Twas brillig, and the slithy toves/Did gyre and gimble in the wabe" because they recognize that there is no pretense of meaning. But when poetry looks as though it ought to make sense, but doesn't—and this is true of much of the poetry published today—readers are turned off. They may feel put down and insulted, may feel small and stupid, may (with spunk) feel angry. But in any case, they will not long pay attention to such poetry.

Therefore, though in this book I am primarily discussing form, you should understand that my overriding concern is with content. I want to help you write effective, comprehensible poetry. Often the devices of poetry, including that basic one, the line break, work against clarity of communication. That is a risk a poet takes in using such devices. But I think a poet has a responsibility to maintain sensitivity to the difficulties such devices make for readers, who are not, after all, technicians. Learn to reach their subconscious with your art, but keep their consciousness in mind. You can't reach readers with anything if you can't keep their attention. As the protagonist (a choreographer) of a brilliant movie, *All That Jazz*, keeps reminding us, "It's show time!" When you start putting words on a page in hopes they will be read, you have to be a showman first. You may be profound or sensitive or inspired or carried away with emotion as well, but it is all futile clowning before the mirror unless you hold the audience glued to their seats.

We don't read poetry to learn facts, and we usually resist it fiercely when it tries too blatantly to tell us how we ought to live our lives. But we respond to it when we are moved. What does that mean—"moved"? It means we become emotionally involved. We experience something.

We feel. We believe the poetry, in the way we believe a gripping novel or movie. How can you, a poet, make your work believable? What has that to do with how you break your lines, how you manage rhythm, how your consonants and vowels echo one another? These are the questions that this book addresses.

And these are questions to which you can learn, if not answers, at least intelligent responses. I write with the assumption that you can learn. I can't teach you to be sensitive, profound, wise, deeply emotional, imaginative, or whatever. I can't teach you to *be* anything. One of the attitudes which most distresses me in the world of poetry today is that some *are* and some are *not* poets, that writing poetry depends more upon the kind of person one is than upon what one has studied and learned. Taken to an extreme, of course, either attitude is ridiculous. There are surely some people who can study for years and still not write good poetry. But when I consider great poets such as Shakespeare or Keats or Yeats or Frost, I know they are more made than born. They studied their craft. They needed that craft in order to release their talent, or inborn ability, to the world. Otherwise they would be trapped like Ariel into a cloven pine without the art of Prospero to release him. I know you agree, or you would not have picked up this book, much less have read this far. You probably know poets who are trying to succeed by sheer force of personality, or what they regard as inspiration. You might have tried that yourself for a while. Many do. But you are probably frustrated by the results, either in your own work or that of other poets winging it on glittering ignorance. Time to learn something. Good. I've been waiting for you to come round.

Some of this material has appeared in slightly different form in my columns in *Writer's Digest,* to which I am grateful for providing me with a continuing forum for the discussion of poetry for over twenty-five years. I hope those who find this book helpful will follow up by reading those columns and *On Being a Poet,* which delves more deeply into topics such as tone, voice, symbolic meaning, and the relation of poetry to the poet's life and to contemporary culture.

1

From Sighs and Groans to Art

Language as a Medium of Art

Anyone can make poetry—and most people do, at least sometimes in their lives. They don't even have to be able to read and write. Poetry is more fundamental than written language. People who live by hunting and gathering in the wilds have poetry in their culture when they have little else that might be recognized as art. Artifacts from a couple of million years ago, found with the remains of our earliest ancestors, include carvings and other indications that art is as old as our species. It is one of the characteristics that define us as human. The words chanted around those prehistoric campfires have not survived, but we may be sure that language has always been a medium for art. Where there are people, there is speech; and where there is speech, there is poetry.

Your very ability to understand these words means you have a highly developed capacity for poetry. Many people bring or send me examples of their writing and ask whether they have a talent for poetry. Without reading their work I can answer: of course they do. But the fact that they come to me with that question is a good indication that they aren't doing much with their talent.

The word *talent* has mystic overtones, suggesting a gift from God to certain favored people. I can give you a talent test right here, one you can administer to yourself. It is based on a principle most creative people recognize. Edison expressed it when he said that invention is 1 percent inspiration and 99 percent perspiration. Let's forget about the 1 percent for a moment and concentrate on the 99.

Talent is mostly motivation, interest, determination, application. When you ask, "Do I have talent?" you can answer yourself with another question: "Am I willing to try?"

I understand why people ask my opinion. They want to save effort. They figure that it would be a waste of time to read, study, practice, develop knowledge and skill, unless there is a likelihood they will have satisfactory results. But the odds are that a person who may eventually write good poetry would be indifferent to such a consideration. He or she would read, study, practice, work at poetry because these activities are satisfying in themselves—regardless of any "results." Asking whether such study is worthwhile is like asking whether it is worthwhile to eat a good meal, or spend time with a loved one, or listen to good music. The reward is in the doing. Good poets never stop learning—and the more they know, the more they are likely to study. But for them that is not work, not something to go through to get results later. They learn because learning is satisfying in itself.

Not everyone has that interest, of course. Do you enjoy picking a poem apart to see how it works? Are you fascinated even by poetry you don't like—as curious about why it doesn't work as you are about why the poetry you do like does work? When you encounter a blind spot in yourself, do you try to figure out why it is there, and whether it can be eliminated? Suppose you can't see what's so great about John Dryden, or William Butler Yeats, or Wallace Stevens, or Dylan Thomas. Do you wonder what you are missing? Are you willing to make an effort to broaden your appreciation?

A primary question (taken up in Chapter 3) is: Do you wonder why the lines are divided the way they are in each poem you read? Do you try to figure out why a poet chose certain words instead of obvious alternatives? Do you recognize tone, the tone of voice: the many shades of humor, wit, sadness, yearning, toughness, anger, tenderness, guardedness that may flicker across a poem? Do you try to discover the poetic devices that create these tones? Do you try to find the focus of each poem you read, its intent, and how the poet went about achieving that intent? Why does the poem begin this way? Why is this material included? Why is so much left unsaid? Why does it end this way? Do you hear the poem as you read it, noticing the way the sounds work together, how the rhythms fall? Do you wonder why poetic styles change so over the centuries, why some kinds of poetry meet human needs in one era and not in another?

That is your talent test. I am not suggesting that you should be able to answer all these questions. But if you find that you are intrigued, that questions such as these seem important, if they make you *want* to know, then, yes, the study of poetry will probably be worthwhile for you. That doesn't mean you'll necessarily get "results," if results mean writing great poetry. The results come as you study, satisfying your curiosity, clarifying your thinking, increasing your knowledge. Your assessment of your own interest is a much more trustworthy guide than my opinion—or anyone else's—of your writing.

One notion you should not worry about is whether you can "be" a poet. You already are one. You were a poet in your crib when you babbled syllables for sheer pleasure, playing with their sounds and rhythms. Because you are human you cannot help being artistic, and because you use language you cannot help using it artfully. But if you think of being a poet as you might think of being a lawyer or welder or ballet dancer, forget it. There really is no such thing; those of us who call ourselves poets mean something else entirely. No one makes a living writing poetry. There is no such thing as a "full-time" poet, as that adjective might be applied to other occupations. Poetry may be quite central to your life, but in economic terms it will be a hobby, not as expensive as trout fishing or photography or needlepoint, but no more likely to pay off, either. It is possible for a writer of prose to make a living sending out work for publication. That is not possible for any poet I know of in modern times (though a few in the past did it). Some poets get jobs—usually as teachers—on the basis of their reputations. Some get fellowships or other kinds of support. Some make a living giving performances of their work. But almost all subsist by other means than poetry, from being supported by their mates, to holding jobs. William Carlos Williams was a doctor. Wallace Stevens was an insurance executive. Many poets are professors. Many are paid well *because* they are poets, but they are not paid well for their writing.

That's probably a good thing. It is even truer of poetry than of the other arts (including prose fiction) that if one writes for the market, writes to sell, the work will be of inferior quality. In Chapter 15, I will discuss in more detail what to do with poems after they are written, but for now—and probably as long as you write poetry—it is probably better simply to put payment out of your mind (and be happy if and when any comes).

As I mentioned in How to Use This Book, poets are made, not born. You should get any notion to the contrary out of your mind. In one sense, as I have said, we are all born poets, but the ability of poets to write well is a skill, acquired like any other. Many are confused about this because poets—deliberately or not—confuse them. The idea that poetry can, indeed should, "just come naturally" is one of the standard themes of poetry. Here is a sixteenth-century sonnet by Sir Philip Sidney which illustrates the point:

> Loving in truth, and fain in verse my love to show,
> That she, dear she, might take some pleasure of my pain,
> Pleasure might cause her read, reading might make her know,
> Knowledge might pity win, and pity grace obtain—
> I sought fit words to paint the blackest face of woe,
> Studying inventions fine, her wits to entertain,
> Oft turning others' leaves to see if thence would flow
> Some fresh and fruitful showers upon my sun-burned brain.
> But words came halting forth, wanting invention's stay;
> Invention, nature's child, fled step-dame Study's blows,
> And others' feet still seemed but strangers in my way.
> Thus, great with child to speak, and helpless in my throes,
>   Biting my truant pen, beating myself for spite
>   Fool, said my muse to me, look in thy heart and write.

That's a good poem—but its meaning is very deceptive. It says, "Look, Ma, no hands!" The poet claims that he studied the classics ("others' leaves") in vain, but was unable to write until he escaped "step-dame Study." Then a voice came from the blue, his muse, telling him to look in his heart and write. Just be sincere. Forget about all that studying. And look what came out! This poem!

Well, the very idea for this poem came from those same classics. It is the trick of any art to make difficult things seem easy and spontaneous: not to *be* sincere but to *seem* sincere. There are many stereotypes of poetry and poets which emphasize the naturalness or the divine origin of poetry, and they are all part of the craftsman's bag of tricks. It should be obvious that no one ever wrote such an intricate, carefully structured, carefully artificial poem as this sonnet of Sidney's simply by looking in his heart and writing. If you believe that, you may believe that rabbits are pulled from empty hats.

Overcoming such illusions should encourage you. You can't do much about inspiration except wait around for the fit to strike—and then probably you won't know what to do with it when it does. Do you think of poets as having especially strong or delicate emotions, of being "sensitive"? No—poets write the poems which convey such feelings. Having the feelings doesn't qualify anyone for anything. It is the craft of getting feelings into the poem which matters. Do you think of poets as profound? I hope not. Profound people are often profound bores. Surely great poetry conveys a sense of divine inspiration, passionate or delicate emotions, deep thoughts, great sincerity, spontaneity, and other qualities. These effects are products of the poet's craft. And it is a craft you can learn.

It helps to stop worrying about what you *are* and concentrate on what you *do.* If you think of a poet as a person with some special qualifications that come by nature (or divine favor), you are likely to make one of two mistakes about yourself. If you think you've got what it takes, you may fail to learn what you need to know in order to use whatever qualities you may have. On the other hand, if you think you do not have what it takes, you may give up too easily, thinking it is useless to try. A poet is someone—you, me, anyone—who writes poems. That question out of the way, now we can learn to write poems better.

When we think of art we usually contrast it with the merely useful or practical. People discovered they could shape clay, bake it at high temperatures, and have useful, durable containers. They also recognized and deliberately created beauty; they shaped and decorated their pots not only for functional but for aesthetic purposes, valuing qualities of form and design (and perhaps associating these with supernatural forces). Apparently an aesthetic sense is instinctual. Just as the beauty of a rose exceeds its function in attracting insects to spread pollen, so human skill always flowers in excess, producing beauty beyond need. Nature is not hardheaded, hardhearted, mechanical, practical, or economical. Neither are we. Our simplest and most practical acts, including the use of language, are likely to be infused with grace and elaboration which utilitarian purposes cannot explain.

In fact, the aesthetic sense may precede the pragmatic. I mentioned the babbling of a baby, the obvious pleasure a child finds in rhythm, rhyme, repetition, variation of pitch, cooing, and gurgling, long before these sounds are used to convey meaning. We might guess that as soon as speech evolved people began making music out of random noise.

Language has two basic functions: expression and communication. First you want to get it out—and then sometimes you want to get it across. At the most rudimentary level the expression is involuntary. You sigh, groan, laugh, cry, scream in terror, or hum with delight. When your circuits are overloaded, you may find relief in verbal discharge. Beyond the mere satisfaction of psychological need, you may create patterns or discover eloquent phrases which are satisfying in themselves. The raw material of poetry may be in whispered sweet nothings or in angry harangues or wails. It may be expressed only to a pillow.

Some of this verbal outpouring is like doodling on a scratch pad, aimless, but with fascinating emerging patterns and shapes. Sometimes we talk to ourselves or write in diaries for the practical purpose of clarifying our feelings, dealing with pain or excitement. But then, as in doodling, we might begin playing around with the possibilities of language—still without any hope or expectation of an audience. It may be that most of the poetry of the world is of this sort, mercifully never exposed to public scrutiny.

But it is the other function of language, communication, we associate with the poetry that gets saved and passed around. In regard to expression, I mentioned both useful and aesthetic aspects. Expression may make you feel better, and it may involve shaping, form, playing around with aesthetic possibilities. Communication also has functional and aesthetic aspects. You may use language to inform people, arouse them, make them think, and so on. And you may use it to give them pleasure or move them by conveying a sense of pattern, shaping, design.

As communication becomes more artistic, its function changes. If you are not only a writer but an artist, you are probably less concerned with conveying what you feel or think than you are with creating an effect on an audience. You use language to make an art object—like a piece of sculpture—which will stand alone. You want your work to be valued for its own sake, not merely for its utilitarian functions such as conveying profundity, sincerity, or information. Some people may read Shakespeare to find out about Shakespeare or about the Renaissance; but if they do so, they are not likely to experience the plays and poems as works of art.

Because we all use language so often to say things or find out things we believe are important, it may be difficult to shift gears and value its artistic dimensions. Great poetry may contain great wisdom, but that is never the reason it is great poetry. It is not enough. It is the form, the shaping of the language, which makes the poetry endure. It is not what it meant to the poet that is important; rather, it is the effect it has on an audience. Art is the creation of effects. This book is intended to help you learn how to create effects. I can't teach you what to think or feel or believe, but I think I can teach you something about how to make your thoughts, feelings, and beliefs into art. The content of poetry, or what it says, may be important, but it is outside the realm of art. The content of some very great poetry may be factually inaccurate, even nonsense, even evil. It may offend you as a person, but you may well appreciate it as an artist.

Some readers, recognizing this, may want to get off our bus right here. They sense—rightly!—that I am talking about distortion of truth, about manipulation of people's feelings, about artificiality. The Puritans in Shakespeare's time demanded the closing of the theaters because they did not approve of lies. Throughout history some people have insisted that language should be used only to convey truth or sincere conviction. They have no patience with fairy tales. If they write verse it is always earnest, moralistic, and devoted to great thoughts in high seriousness.

Others who may want off the bus are not Puritans at all. We might call them Pantheists—people who worship nature. It seems unnatural to twist words around to make art out of them. They want to let it all hang out, tell it like it is, and if we object that their poetry is sloppy or dull or redundant or nonsensical or disgusting, they are likely to reply that this is how it came out, that is how they felt, that's real, that's natural.

Neither Puritans nor Pantheists are likely to learn much from this book. Art *is* artificial. That's what the word means—altering nature. It is also true that poetry, in a way, is lying. It may contain great truths about human nature, about life, about society. It may create characters who seem more real than you or I. It is often realistic; the world it pictures looks like the world we live in. But truth in great poetry is always expressed by indirection. Robert Frost compared the way truth looks in poetry to the way a stick looks in water. The word *poet* means "maker." The poet creates realities.

And good poetry manipulates the audience, as does a play or a magician. Poetry requires more showmanship than honesty. Readers who understand this do not resent it. They enjoy the performance, recognizing and appreciating the skill. Some naive readers (and poets) take the mumbo jumbo and dramatics of poetry too literally. When they find out how poetry really works they are likely to be disillusioned—as a child is disillusioned finding out about Santa Claus. But if your artistic instincts are strong, and you like to write, you will be as thrilled by the pleasure of making things up as you will be by using language with precision and beauty.

You can best understand the nature of poetry by comparing it to other arts. For example, though much poetry seems highly personal and autobiographical, very little actually represents the thoughts, feelings, or circumstances of the life of the poet. Like science, poetry has a kind of impersonality. A great work of art, like a great scientific truth, stands alone. The creator cannot come running along behind explaining and tidying up like an anxious parent.

For example, Whitman's "Song of Myself" has a blatantly egoistic title, but you will read it in vain for much insight into Walt the man. Where is Chaucer in the massive fiction of *The Canterbury Tales?* Where is Milton in *Paradise Lost?* Shakespeare in *Hamlet?* Sometimes the poet uses himself as a character in his work, as Dante does in *The Divine Comedy,* but that is a fiction, too. When you see a poem written in the first person, it is safest to assume that the "I" is an invented character, as in a drama—a deliberate and artificial creation who may or may not accurately resemble the poet who made it up.

The comparison with drama (and drama's requirement of showmanship) is useful in other ways. There are three major genres, or kinds, of poetry: **dramatic, narrative,** and **lyric** (see Chapter 9). Poetry in the dramatic mode is the most immediate. It seems to put the action before your very eyes, as does a play. A narrative is a somewhat more distant form. It tells a story, and in doing so may summarize action rather than representing it, though in its climactic "scenes" the poet usually dramatizes, just as in a play, giving the words of various speakers and telling what they are doing right at the moment. Most poetry you see published today is in the third mode, lyric. Originally a lyric was a poem to be sung to a lyre (an ancient stringed instrument). We still call the words of songs *lyrics*. But the word has been expanded to mean any relatively short poem which expresses personal thought and feeling, or seems to do so. It implies one voice, usually speaking in the first person. But, as I have mentioned, it is safest to interpret even a lyric as a speech from a play, assuming the "I" to be fictional.

Lyric suggests the association of poetry and music. Many verse dramas include songs. Narratives (such as epics) were often chanted, sometimes to the rhythmic beat of drums or other instruments. The most fundamental element of poetic form is the line, which may be related to the timing of music. Poetry was an oral (or spoken) art long before it was ever written, and the shading between spoken and sung performance is subtle, very much a matter of degree. If you hear recordings of such great poets as William Butler Yeats, E. E. Cummings, T. S. Eliot, or Dylan Thomas reading their work, you will hear how their voices shade toward song, and even though the rasping voice of Robert Frost might seem anything but musical, the regularity of cadence and interworking of sounds give his poetry a musical dimension (which might be compared to the lyrics known as "talking blues").

However, we most commonly encounter poetry today in its written form, which is unfortunate, for in some ways a written poem is like a musical score, a set of instructions for performers, and many readers cannot "hear" the poem as they read, any more than they can imagine musical notes as they would sound in performance. As we move further and further from the oral culture of earlier times, we miss more and more of poetry's music.

But there are some compensations, since poetry develops relationships to the visual arts (those intended to be viewed) or graphic arts (those, such as painting, which use flat surfaces). Some of the effects of poetry today are meant for the eye rather than for the ear. To some extent this has been true ever since poetry began appearing in print. Some seventeenth-century poems are **acrostics**—the first letters of each line (or the last letters, or both) spell out significant words. Other poems were written in the shape of wings, altars, Christmas trees, or other objects.

Some modern poets have gone farther toward the graphic arts, writing poems to be read, not heard. This one by E. E. Cummings cannot be read aloud at all:

<pre>
            l(a

            l e

            af

            fa

            l l

            s)

            one

            l

            iness
</pre>

The poem plays on the fact that a figure one looks like a small letter *l*. There is a *one* buried in *loneliness*. There are also a couple of *l*'s. The last two letters of *leaf* happen to be reversed in the first two of *falls,* an accident which may have suggested to the poet the twisting of a falling leaf. The typographic arrangement brings attention to these curiosities. The statement, or meaning, of the poem is an interwoven clause, "A leaf falls," and a word, "loneliness." Separate them and you have a very short, rather Japanese poem: "A leaf falls: loneliness."

Such tricks are exceptions in the work of Cummings, most of whose poetry is in quite conventional forms (in spite of its unconventional punctuation and spacing). The graphic element in poetry is a kind of aberration from its main traditions, but an interesting one. In 1956, in Brazil, some artist-poets invented a complete melding of graphic art and poetry. They called it **concrete poetry.** The kind and size of type, even the color of the ink, and the exact arrangement of the words on the page (as in a poster) are all part of the effect of the poem. Individual letters, words, marks of punctuation, or other symbols of written communication are used in concrete poetry as visual objects—in addition to or instead of their function in communicating language.

Concrete poetry is an extreme, practiced by few today. But you can count on artists to try the limits of their medium, to push things as far as they will go. Is the basic unit of poetry the line? Some poets defy that principle and write **prose poems,** intense passages, usually in paragraph form, that have all the characteristics of the lyric except that they don't use lines. There is a popular association of poetry with beautiful language, imaginative figures of speech, elevating thoughts. So some poets deliberately use the ugliest language they can find, avoid figures of speech entirely, or dwell on shocking themes. A line usually represents a measure of some sort, some number of units (in some ways like a bar in music). So, naturally, poets began writing lines which were not measured, calling it free verse. (Robert Frost said contemptuously that writing free verse was like playing tennis with the net down, but he nonetheless wrote some fine free verse!) If you are inclined to test limits, you will find few in poetry that haven't been tested thoroughly.

There are no rules. You can call anything you want a poem, and the Bureau of Standards won't say a word. One young poet I knew included the sound of a roller windowshade rattling up (as when you jerk it and release the string) in one of his poems. He had to have such a shade available to perform the poem. I don't know what has happened to him or his poem. That type of shade is rapidly going out of style.

But there are also strong, stable traditions in poetry, and after playing around the edges with experimental possibilities, most serious poets settle down to fairly predictable forms. In spite of perpetual revolution in the arts, which sometimes makes them seem like spinning wheels, the iambic pentameter line (explained in Chapter 5) used for their best work by Chaucer, Shakespeare, Milton, Dryden, Pope, Browning, Frost, Robinson, and most of the other major English and American poets, is still the most common line used by major poets writing in English. There are good reasons for this, which I will explain in later chapters. Among other things it indicates that however much artists like to rebel and experiment and try new things, they are also inclined to be traditionalists, with a respect for, almost a devotion to, the artistic monuments that have come before them.

That devotion is particularly appropriate for poetry, for it is the art most often cited as the core of civilization, past and present. In spite of all its tricks, postures, gimmicks, paradoxes, and devices, it remains the central repository of the values and aspirations of a culture. That's a long way from sighs and groans. Welcome to the temple.

2

Well of English Undefiled

Diction

If you were a potter, clay would be your medium. You would know the many varieties of clay, what stresses and strains they can take, what happens to them under various conditions and temperatures. Similarly, your work as a poet requires you to understand how language works—and, specifically, to know the peculiarities of English.

"Peculiarities" is the right word for the characteristics of our language. English derives its strength and beauty from its strange history. We have all grumbled about the way our spelling makes no sense. It is not phonetic. Someone (I think Bernard Shaw) once said we could spell *fish* with the letters *ghoti*, pronouncing the *gh* as in *enough*, the *o* as in *women*, and *ti* as in *nation*. These oddities in spelling and similar oddities in grammar are primarily the result of a forced wedding of a Latinate language with a Germanic one after the Norman Conquest of England in 1066.

Before the Norman French conquered them, the natives of England spoke a variety of dialects related to German. Collectively, these dialects formed a language which is now referred to as Old English (or Anglo-Saxon), the language of *Beowulf*. Germanic languages represent one branch of a family of languages derived from a prehistoric language known as Indo-European (because most of the languages of Europe and a number of Asian languages are in this family). Another branch of

Indo-European is represented by Latin and the languages derived from Latin (the Romance languages—Italian, Spanish, French, etc.). Germanic languages and Romance languages are, therefore, rather like cousins, whereas French and Spanish, or Old English and German, are more like brothers and sisters. The Normans were of Viking stock (their name means "northmen"), but they had settled in that part of France which came to be called Normandy. When they conquered England they brought with them French language and culture and imposed it on the native English. This mating of cousins resulted in the bastard language we know as English.

Edmund Spenser, in *The Faerie Queene* (1589), spoke of the first great poet in the new language, Chaucer, as "a well of English undefiled." The tribute was just—but misleading. Chaucer's greatness rested in large part upon his ability (at the end of the fourteenth century) to make a smooth mixture out of German water and French oil.

More than half our vocabulary comes from Latin, either directly or through French. The French, after all, were the ruling class: their language—and later borrowings from Latin—dominated business, theology, philosophy and scholarship, government and the affairs of state. But then, as now, most people had little to do with such formal concerns in their everyday lives. Most of our gutsy, familiar, everyday words are of Germanic origin. We have parallel vocabularies of common words and formal ones. You can see these two levels or strains in the following lists. The words on the left are of Germanic origin; those on the right derive from Latin:

house	residence
sweat	perspiration
work	labor
food	comestibles
walk	perambulate
hug	embrace
dog	canine

One list contains the words of common speech, the other a vocabulary appropriate for formal occasions. Such pairs of words exist for almost anything we wish to express. Can you add half a dozen to each? It is as though we were fluent in two languages. When I was in Latin class, I had to memorize the following sentence: "Persons residing in crystalline structures should refrain from capitulating lapidary fragments." That is Latinate English for "People who live in glass houses shouldn't throw stones." Such Latinate language sounds to most of us as Norman French must have sounded to the Anglo-Saxons: rather pompous and formal. It's the way we peasants had to talk when we addressed the lord of the manor, the sheriff, the priest, the fancy-dressed merchants. It is book language, not the familiar tongue heard around the hearth.

Which is the better language for poetry? Obviously we have to use both, but as poets we have to have greater than usual sensitivity to the emotional effects of language. Many poets develop a fondness for the etymological references in the dictionary—those little abbreviations and early forms which trace the history of words. Look up *hug,* for instance. My desk dictionary says "perh. of Scand. origin; akin to ON *hugga* to soothe." The Scandinavian languages are cognates of English— like brothers and sisters. "ON" in that dictionary entry refers to Old Norse. In an etymological reference book I get a somewhat fuller explanation: "ON *hugga,* to comfort or soothe, as a mother hugging her child: prob. orig. echoic from the comforting words or sounds of a lullaby." I like to imagine a Viking mother making *hugga* sounds as she rocks her restless babe.

Let's compare the Latinate equivalent—*embrace.* The root is the Latin word for arm (as in French *bras,* Spanish *brazo*). To embrace is to take into one's two arms. That is a vivid image; but the connotations of the two words, *hug* and *embrace,* are very different, largely because of the origins of the words. *Hug* has a motherly, affectionate, intimate feeling about it. *Embrace* can be either more formal (as a general embraces a soldier) or more passionate. I think a man might be more likely to hug than to embrace his sister. Hugging seems both more sexually innocent and more familial. "She hugged me." "She embraced me." These are different actions with different overtones. The connotations of the words have been formed by their histories. Which word is right for your poem? You may find yourself using the dictionary even for very familiar words to find out more about them. One thing a poet learns is that there is no such thing as a synonym. Each word has irrepressible individuality.

Language begins in the concrete, develops into the abstract. A **concrete** word is one which is close to experience—to something you can imagine (a verb formed from the noun *image*). An **abstract** word speaks more to the mind than to the senses. "He was pitching around on the bed, frothing at the mouth, babbling nonsense, his skin hot as a skillet." That language is concrete. It helps the reader see, hear, feel, experience. "He was delirious." That sentence is abstract. It summarizes, speaks to the mind. Usually poetry attempts to create experience, so its language is likely to be concrete; but there are occasions for abstractions in poetry as well. Therefore you must be able to use both kinds of language skillfully.

Latinate words in English have lost their vividness. *Delirious* was a very concrete word for the ancient Romans. It means "out of the furrow," implying the image of a plow having jumped the straight row. But a reader of modern English is not likely to know that, and the word seems abstract to us. Abstract language tends to be weaker than concrete language; it has less emotional impact. Which is stronger: "You lie!" or "You prevaricate!"? *Prevaricate,* like *delirious,* held an image for the Romans. It meant walking crooked, knock-kneed. But that concrete, experiential flavor has been lost. For readers of modern English, the Germanic word *lie* comes through with greater force.

Words of Latin origin tend to be longer—to have more syllables—than do words of Germanic origin. Overused, Latinate words fill the mouth but actually provide little to chew. Syllables are expensive for poets. You learn to spend them like dollars. *Disestablishmentarianism* is a ten-dollar word. It would take up a whole line of iambic pentameter (if it were iambic, which it isn't—as you will learn in subsequent chapters).

Poets learn to use Latinate words carefully and to set them like jewels. Can you pick out the Latinate words in these opening lines of Karl Shapiro's "Auto Wreck"?

> Its quick soft silver bell beating, beating,
> And down the dark one ruby flare
> Pulsing out red light like an artery,
> The ambulance at top speed floating down
> Past beacons and illuminated clocks
> Wings in a heavy curve, dips down,
> And brakes speed, entering the crowd.

Artery and *ambulance* are Latinate. There are no Old English equivalents. This is true of most scientific terms. People in Western culture tend to go to Latin or Greek to invent names for new phenomena. For example, the French called a field hospital a "walking hospital," or *hôpital ambulant*—which is why our word for a swift car comes from a Latin word for "walking." *Ambulance* falls into place in this poem with neat power, explaining what the opening imagery is all about. *Pulsing* comes from a Latin root, but is short and unpretentious—and better than Germanic alternatives such as *beating* (which the poet had already used) or *throbbing,* because it so clearly associates the red light of the ambulance with arterial bleeding. *Illuminated* is Latinate. The Old English equivalent would be *lighted,* which the poet may have avoided because he had already used *light.* But *illuminated* is appropriate anyway to suggest the loftiness and oblivious authority of the clocks. *Entering,* like *pulsing,* is so familiar that, though of Latin origin, it seems domesticated. *Splitting* would be a Germanic alternative, but *entering* makes the crowd seem like a building, opening and closing around the ambulance in a hush. The other significant words in the passage are of Germanic origin. You will find this true of most good poetry: Latinate words are used sparingly and each is deliberately, carefully placed.

The final strophe of the poem raises philosophical, abstract questions—and the language is appropriately more Latinate:

> Already old, the question Who shall die?
> Becomes unspoken Who is innocent?
> For death in war is done by hands;
> Suicide has cause and stillbirth, logic;
> And cancer, simple as a flower, blooms.
> But this invites the occult mind,
> Cancels our physics with a sneer,
> And spatters all we knew of denouement
> Across the expedient and wicked stones.

Here it is the Germanic words which stand out—those such as *blooms, sneer, spatters,* and *stones.* The pair of adjectives in the last line is striking: the Latinate *expedient,* the Germanic *wicked. Expedient* has the root meaning of freeing one's foot—as from a trap. Here it is used ironically: those stones certainly do their job well, are well suited to the task of spattering a body. Irony involves wit, a kind of intellectual humor (which is not necessarily funny), a highly sophisticated kind of comment to which a Latinate word, with its touch of pomposity, is quite appropriate (or expedient). *Wicked* is at the other end of the scale—almost primitive, a kind of curse on the stones.

Excellent **diction,** or choice of words, which the last line of Shapiro's poem illustrates, is for most readers or critics perhaps the first mark of talent. When one senses that a poet is choosing words carefully, imaginatively, with a deep sense of their rightness (based on, among other things, a sense of their history), he has confidence in the poet as a passenger has confidence in a good driver. Convinced of the poet's care and control in the use of language, the reader can release his mind to experience the art of the poem. You can easily test this. Take an example from one of your favorite poets. Sort out the Latinate and Germanic words and look up the etymologies of words that seem strikingly appropriate. Is your respect for the poet in part based upon an unconscious recognition of loving control of language?

So far I have talked primarily about the meaning of words and their connotations, as affected by the mingling of Latinate and Germanic elements in English. But that mingling had important effects on spelling and grammar as well. Some peculiarities of spelling result from our pronouncing Latinate words in Germanic ways. Many of our silent letters (such as the *b* in *debt*) were pronounced in the languages from which the words came. (*Debt* comes from Latin *debere;* the word came into Middle English from French *dette,* and the *b* was later introduced into the spelling by scholars who recognized the Latin root, though speakers of English did not pronounce it.)

English tends to shift accents forward, so final syllables tend to be slurred. If you have studied French or Spanish, you know that a word such as *admiration,* in those languages spelled with a *c* instead of a *t,* is pronounced with a stress on the final syllable: *ahd-mee-rah-see-OWN.* When we shift the stress forward, to the *RA,* as in English, the last two syllables are run together, and we have the odd spelling of the *ti* or *ci* for what is pronounced as *sh.* Some reformers have suggested that we change to a more phonetic spelling: something like *admurayshun.* But I hope all poets will resist such fiddling with our language's evolutionary development. The richness and flexibility of our language has produced a variety of accents and dialects which would be lost if spelling were standardized, thus impelling everyone to pronounce words the same way. How would we spell *tomato? Tumaytoh* or *tumahtoh?* It may seem simpler to spell both *knight* and *night* as *nite*—but what a wealth of associations would be lost! *Night,* a Germanic word, still expresses its cousinship with Latin *nox.* And *knight*—a different word entirely—is related to *kin* and *king* and to German *knecht,* meaning servant. Part of the excitement of rhyming in English is juxtaposition of words which look as different as *bluff* and *enough.* Sensitivity to the ancient roots and to the stubborn individuality of words is an important indication of poetic ability.

But the most radical effect of our blending of cousin languages is not on meaning or spelling, but on grammar. Both Latin and German are highly inflected languages, as are all the European languages derived from them. **Inflection** means the change of form in a word to express a change in meaning. We say *she* when the pronoun is the subject of a sentence or clause, but *her* when it is an object. We change the form of most words to express plurals—adding an *s,* or changing the spelling (as from *child* to *children*). The change from *is* to *are* to *was,* or *look* to *looks* to *looked* illustrates inflection. But, in spite of these examples, English is a lightly inflected language. The inflections of the Germanic and Latinate languages got mixed up and eventually were abandoned altogether. As in Chinese and a few other languages, it is word order which primarily determines meaning in English.

In Latin, *Puer puellam amat* means "The boy loves the girl." Arrange the words as you will—*puellam puer amat, puellam amat puer*—and the forms of the nouns tell you which is doing the loving and which is loved; any arrangement means "The boy loves the girl." If you want to say "The girl loves the boy," you have to change the forms of the nouns, making the word for boy accusative, *puerum,* and that for girl nominative, *puella.* Since we have no nominative and accusative case for nouns in English, we express the difference by word order. The noun before the verb is the subject, and the noun after the verb is the direct object. Usually! But who is Suzy? The girl the boy loves. Loves the girl the boy? Yes, the girl the boy loves. Though these sentences are not normal in English, they still make sense and make possible a number of subtle shadings. Suppose we make a grammatical error: "Him loves she." That sentence may pain the ear, but we still know what it means—that a masculine person loves a feminine person—because the word order is more important than the inflections. The Latin equivalent *Eum amat ea* means the opposite—a feminine person loves a masculine person.

In the Caribbean islands today, we can hear language in transition, much as it might have changed in England during the eleventh century. Conquering speakers of English are imposing their language on a variety of African dialects, Spanish, Dutch, and several other tongues. The result is an amalgam sometimes called Calypso. In Calypso even the few inflections we have in English are disappearing. Present tenses may be used for past tenses: *he go* might mean "he went." The *s* on plurals and possessives is often dropped: *he wear shoe* might mean "he wears shoes." Or it might mean "she wears shoes." You have to determine meaning from context. When my wife had twins, the Harvard-educated doctor announced, after the first, "He a girl," then, after the second, "He a girl, too." A student wrote in a college composition, "He hit he with he," meaning (I could tell from the context) "She hit him with it." *He* has become an all-purpose pronoun, used for *he, she, it, him, her.*

What difference does all this make to poets? In the first place, if language is to be the medium of your art, you must have some sense of how language works, get over the idea that there are right and wrong ways to say things, and begin to feel the infinite possibilities language contains. But it is also important that you understand the unique richness and flexibility of English—as well as its ambiguity and the problems it offers to foreigners who try to learn it. In the seventeenth century the English poet John Dryden said that when he wanted to make sure a paragraph made sense he translated it into Latin and then back into English. Latin is a much more exact language than English. In many ways French and German and other European languages are clearer, more precise than English. But none of these languages has the wealth of association and bewildering variety of English—the qualities which help create the beauty and depth of our poetry. If you have the kind of mind which demands logic and certainty, elimination of haziness and paradox, predictability and clear definition, try mathematics. If you have a mind for poetry, you will take delight in the very qualities of language which frustrate and perplex people who expect language to be reasonable.

Yet there is a logic in the language itself to which a poet must always be true. The opening of "The Windhover," by Gerard Manley Hopkins, is bewildering on first reading:

> I caught this morning morning's minion, king-
>> dom of daylight's dauphin, dapple-dawn-drawn Falcon, in
>> his riding
> Of the rolling level underneath him steady air, and striding
> High there, how he rung upon the rein of a wimpling wing
> In his ecstasy! then off, off forth on swing,
>> As a skate's heel sweeps smooth on a bow-bend: the hurl and
>> gliding
> Rebuffed the big wind. My heart in hiding
> Stirred for a bird—the achieve of, the mastery of the thing!

But these are rather straightforward English sentences, true to the inner necessity of the language. The subject of the first is "I," the verb is "caught." What did I catch? The minion (or servant) of the morning, who is also the dauphin (or prince) of the kingdom of daylight. What is this minion, this dauphin? It is a falcon. What kind of a falcon? One drawn by the dapple dawn. (Notice how that phrase requires you to emphasize the word *dawn: dapple-DAWN-drawn.* The sense is less clear if you say *DAPple-dawn-drawn* or *dapple-dawn-DRAWN.*) I caught him in his riding of the steady air which was rolling level underneath him. And while he was striding high there, I was amazed by the way he rung upon the rein of a wimpling wing. The word "rung" might be puzzling to you. It makes no sense if you think of it in terms of ringing a bell. Think of ringing a maypole—going round it. In library dictionaries you will discover that *ring* in this sense had a special meaning for falconry. When a bird spirals upward it is ringing, going round. *Rein* (as in the reins of a bridle) is a controlling force, something that checks, holds back. To *wimple* is to ripple or to curve. How the falcon spiraled upward controlled by a rippling wing! Hopkins, a Jesuit priest, may also have had in mind the image of a nun's wimple, which looks like bird wings.

Then he was off, off, swinging forth in an arc like that of the heel of an ice skate cutting a bow-like bend. The bird could hurl itself and glide in a way that seemed to repel the big wind. (*Rebuff* literally means "to puff back at.") My heart was hidden within me, but it was stirred by the bird, its achievement, its mastery over the material universe.

Reading poetry as dense as this requires constant use of the diction-
ary, almost as though one were translating from a foreign language,
partly because Hopkins, writing in the late nineteenth century,
deliberately used archaic words and current words in archaic senses. He
was infatuated with the richness of the language and wrung every bit of
meaning he could out of it. But once you have the meaning of the poem
clearly in mind, go back over those lines, reading them aloud, and listen
to their music. (Notice, for instance, the five stresses per line: those lines
are the octave of a Petrarchan sonnet! In Chapters 4 and 10 I will refer
you to this poem to study its accentual meter and sonnet form.) What
looks at first like a tortured distortion of the language is, once you
understand it, a testament to the language's inner strength and beauty.

You probably don't want to write like Hopkins—and I doubt that you
or I could. Poets such as Hopkins emphasize artifice in the way they use
language. Others emphasize naturalness of idiom. Robert Frost's
"Directive" begins with the line: "Back out of all this now too much for
us," a line which may be as bewildering on first reading as the opening of
the poem by Hopkins, though it is composed entirely of simple, one-
syllable words. You have to hear it, imagine it conversationally, to make
sense of it. See if the succeeding lines help:

> Back out of all this now too much for us,
> Back in a time made simple by the loss
> Of detail, burned, dissolved, and broken off
> Like graveyard marble sculpture in the weather,
> There is a house that is no more a house
> Upon a farm that is no more a farm
> And in a town that is no more a town.

The blurring of meaning in that first line is apparently deliberate, as
though the poet were withholding clarity until the comparison to
graveyard sculpture falls into place to help you imagine just the sort of
worn and damaged simplicity he is talking about.

I said in the last chapter that artists tend to strain things to the limits.
Hopkins strained in one direction, Frost in the opposite. Hopkins tried
to dig up words which had become rare through disuse, to capture some
of the power and rhythm and vocabulary of Old English poetry, and to

bring vitality back to the lost imagery of Latin roots. Frost seemed to be challenged by the most common and colorless words of ordinary conversation. I use the term **business words** for the little, necessary, but generally dull, words required by grammar and conversational ease—such words as *of, in, the, a, this, that.* Frost made poetry out of these words, using them in conversational twists that focused attention on them and made them seem fresh and new. His best lines are often made up entirely of words without any imagistic force, words used in such a way as to light up themselves and penetrate to wisdom, as when a husband and wife, in "The Death of the Hired Man," contrast their definitions of "home":

> "Home is the place where, when you have to go there,
> They have to take you in."
> > "I should have called it
> Something you somehow haven't to deserve."

One could make a similar contrast between the poetry of Dylan Thomas and W. H. Auden. Like Hopkins, Thomas used a rich, thumping, often difficult language which draws attention to itself, shimmers with color and life. Auden, like Frost, leaned toward the conversational, using a language often as colorless and pure as water, deriving its power from the unexpected lifting of the commonplace into art.

Every good poet uses language in some distinctive way. Poets are able to do this because they saturate themselves in English, tuning their sensibilities to all its twists and turns and special peculiarities, both historical and current. They play with its sounds and meanings and arrangements. Unless you share that fascination with language for its own sake and, especially, with the sometimes incredible oddities of English, the ways in which it is like no other language on earth, you are not likely to become an effective poet.

Cliche, or the use of overused, exhausted (and often rather pretentious) phrases, is the antithesis of poetry. When a reader senses that a writer is so indifferent to language that he can use a cliche such as "golden dawn," or a **tautology** such as "distant sky," or a **hackneyed** or **trite** phrase such as John Dean's famous "at this point in time," or indulge in wordiness such as "for the reason that" (instead of "because"), the reader loses confidence and respect. To hear someone abuse language is like listening to music written by a composer indifferent to harmonies, rhythms, and tones.

I must renew the warning of the last chapter. If you are so concerned with *what* you say that you don't care *how* you say it, you will not write effective poetry. The first mark of a bad poet is any indication that he or she is so involved with meaning that form is neglected. Suppose that you love someone passionately and sincerely. You write, "I can't tell you how much I love you. It is more than I can say." Those words may have been intended to convey a great deal of feeling, but they are pretty flat on the page. If you cannot figure out some way to pump life into the language, you may deserve credit as an honest person, but you will get none for being an artist.

Sometimes I see poems with a single word, such as

God

set off on a line by itself, an indication that the writer thinks God is very important and perhaps wants to draw attention to his importance. Well, that may be advertising (though not very effective advertising), but the message dominates the art. If you feel terrible, you have to find some more original way to say it than "I feel terrible." If you hate war, you have to find some better way to say it than General Sherman's "War is Hell!" Such expressions may use language, but they fail to get inside it, to discover and illuminate its inner strength and necessity, its strange beauty. They are not art.

3

Breaking Sense

Line Division; Cadenced Poetry; Syllabic and
Quantitative Meters

The violent yoking of a Germanic and a Latinate language which
resulted in what we know as English—with our strange spelling, gram-
mar, and vocabulary—also produced a hybrid metrical form. **Meter**
means measurement, specifically the measurement of line length. If you
write poetry, as opposed to prose, you choose to write in lines (unless
you write prose poems, which are poetic paragraphs that do not employ
the line as a unit). Where do you divide those lines and why? This is the
fundamental question you have to ask yourself as a poet. If you have no
answer for it, why not write prose?

The answers that poets have come up with in various societies and
languages and historical eras reflect their whole cultural background,
especially the nature of the language they write in. The northern Ger-
manic tribes brought one kind of metrical system to England. When the
French-speaking Normans conquered England in 1066 they brought a
different kind of metrical system. Neither system was quite appropriate
to the new language which emerged as a blend of the two. The charac-
teristic forms of poetry in English came to be in an entirely unique metri-
cal system reflecting the mixed nature of the language itself. Our meter is
puzzling, difficult, mysterious—and rich with possibilities.

We have talked about how art necessarily distorts its medium. Art is
artificial. The excitement and beauty of art arise from a tension, or pull-

ing, or interplay, between form and content, between the shape the artist gives the work and the medium used. So it is with language used in the art of poetry. The tensions between the Germanic and Latinate elements of the language help keep the poetry alive. And the tensions in metrical form also help make it thump and squirm with vitality.

First, let's look at the various ways of dividing lines.

> One way
> of doing that
> would be
> to break the line
> at the ends
> of phrases
> for easy comprehension.

Do these line breaks make the sentence easier to read? Some writers have thought so. A pair of scientists wrote a popular book on relativity in lines like that, breaking the meaning into small bites for easy chewing. Line breaks that coincide with natural pauses or units of meaning—phrases or sentences or single words set off for emphasis—are called **rhetorical.** One meaning of **rhetoric,** as opposed to **form,** is a concern with meaning. Form and meaning can never be absolutely separated, but they can be made to tug against one another, to seem at odds.

Rhetorical line breaks generally make for rather dull poetry. If the broken lines above are regarded as poetry at all, they would have to be called free verse. **Free verse** uses lines that are of any length the poet chooses, without any set measure (or meter). Many free-verse poets of the early part of this century used primarily rhetorical line breaks, as in this passage from Amy Lowell's "Lilacs," a poem you will find in most anthologies of American literature:

> Lilacs,
> False blue,
> White,
> Purple,
> Color of lilac,
> Your great puffs of flowers
> Are everywhere in this my New England.

Each line comes to a nearly dead stop. Suppose she had done it this way:

    Lilacs, false
    blue, white, purple, color of
    lilac, your great
    puffs of
    flowers are
    everywhere in
    this my New
    England.

I won't call that an improvement. (I'm not sure the lines can be much improved.) But the lines are deliberately broken in such a way as to tug against the meaning. They keep jerking you around the corner to complete the phrases rather than letting you rest at the ends of phrases. This device is called **enjambment,** or the use of **runover lines.** Enjambment is a matter of degree; some lines are enjambed more sharply, or violate the sense more dramatically, than others. For instance, to separate "New" from "England" cuts right into the center of a term. This brings fresh attention to the term. My new what? My New England. There is a tendency to pause momentarily at the ends of lines, to linger on the last syllable. (One poet called it the pause of half a comma.) For an instant, as you wonder what "New" applies to, your mind is opened as it would not be by the familiar, closed phrase "New England."

Closure, or the use of closed lines, resolves **tension.** Enjambment heightens tension. As an artist you are not merely concerned with getting your meaning across, or you would just write expository prose. You want to generate interest and involvement with the language as well as with what it says. Another way of putting it would be to say you want a deeper meaning than is conveyed by the mere denotation of the words. Such meaning includes emotion, a response, a caring, which you can convey by sometimes rubbing language against its grain. For each line you write you want to decide whether closure, and ease of tension, or enjambment, and sharpening of tension, is appropriate for your purposes, the purposes of the poem.

What we call a **line** in poetry may be more than a line on the printed page. It is a unit of composition. You probably recognize the source of these lines:

> He shall come down like rain upon the mown grass: as showers
>   that water the earth.
> In his days shall the righteous flourish: and abundance of
>   peace so long as the moon endureth.
> He shall have dominion also from sea to sea, and from the
>   river unto the ends of the earth.
> They that dwell in the wilderness shall bow before him; and
>   his enemies shall lick the dust.

That poetry was written in ancient Hebrew and translated into English by a group of scholars assembled by King James I of England in the early seventeenth century. It comes from Psalm 72.

Are the lines closed or enjambed? Each is not only closed, but is a complete sentence. Yet they are not like the sentences of prose. They have been carefully shaped by the poet. Notice the pause in the middle of each. Such a pause in a line of poetry is called a **caesura.** The caesuras in this passage are clearly deliberate parts of the structure of each line (or of each "verse," as lines in the Bible are customarily called). There is a kind of **balance** between the concepts or images on one side of the caesura and those on the other. Sometimes, as in the last line, the balance is a contrast or **antithesis;** the first part relates to the faithful, and the second to those who reject God.

You may notice another kind of balancing going on as well. In this translation, at least, there tend to be approximately the same number of strong stresses, or **accents,** on each side of the caesura:

> he shall come DOWN like RAIN upon the mown GRASS;
> as SHOWers that WATer the EARTH.

Do you hear similar patterns in the other lines? I will discuss stress in greater detail later, but, for the moment, notice that it suggests a different kind of possibility for line division. Such a balance is **formal,** rather than rhetorical. Some counting is going on—at least in a loose way. The poet (or translator) wants the reader to be sensitive to the music of the language as well as to its meaning. Poetry that is organized by balanced phrases and a loose regularity of strong stresses is sometimes called **cadenced.** The cadences of biblical poetry are so sonorous that at times they drown out altogether our awareness of what the words are saying.

The King James Version of the Bible has had a strong influence on our poetry. These lines sound as though they might have been taken from a Psalm:

> I hear and behold God in every object, yet I understand
>   God not in the least,
> Nor do I understand who there can be more wonderful
>   than myself . . .
> Why should I wish to see God better than this day?
> I see something of God each hour of the twenty-four,
>   and each moment then,
> In the faces of men and women I see God, and in my own face
>   in the glass;
> I find letters from God dropped in the street, and every one is
>   signed by God's name,
> And I leave them where they are, for I know that others will
>   punctually come forever and ever.

That is Walt Whitman, in "Song of Myself." His poetry is not always this regular, but there tends to be the strong caesura and balancing of strong stresses that we saw in the Psalm.

When you decide to write poetry rather than prose you want to figure out how to make the language resonate. When tension goes out of the writing, the language sags like a slack string on a guitar. How do you pull it tight? When do you want the slackness, when the tension? These are the questions you are constantly working with as a poet. How do you give your lines a lift?

That word **lift** is another technical term. The tendency in English is to move accents forward—toward the beginning of words or phrases. When we string words together in normal speech or prose writing, the energy bunches up and trails off. Every fourth or fifth syllable gets a stress—like a Saturday night bath, whether it needs it or not—and many stresses which would be pronounced in isolated words are slurred over. Here is a passage of prose criticism written by the poet Delmore Schwartz (the one who supplied the inspiration for Saul Bellow's novel *Humboldt's Gift*). I have indicated the syllables I stress when reading it aloud. Notice that they are not necessarily the syllables which are important in terms of what the words are saying:

> SOME poetry employs beLIEFS merely as an ASpect of the
> THOUGHTS and eMOtions of the human CHARacters with
> which it is conCERNED. almost EVery draMAtic poet will serve
> as an exAMple of this TENdency. human beings are FULL of
> beliefs, a fact which EVen the naturalistic NOvelist cannot wholly
> forGET; and since their beLIEFS are very important MOtives in
> their LIVES, no SERious poet can forGET about beLIEFS all the
> TIME. one DOUBTS that any serious POet would want to DO so.

You might put the stresses in somewhat different places, and so might I
on another reading, but in reading prose we adopt a rhythm in which
stresses fall with approximately this frequency.

Let's compare that with a passage of the same author's poetry, with
stresses indicated in the same way:

> in the NAKed BED, in PLAto's CAVE,
> reFLECTed HEADlights SLOWly SLID the WALL,
> CARpenters HAMmered UNder the SHADed WINdow,
> WIND TROUBled the WINdow CURtains ALL NIGHT LONG,
> a FLEET of TRUCKS STRAINED upHILL, GRINDing,
> their FREIGHTS COVered, as USual.
> the CEILing LIGHTened aGAIN, the SLANTing DIagram
> SLID SLOWly FORTH.

The first thing you notice when you compare these passages is that the
poetry has many more stresses than the prose. This is primarily because
the poet uses more syllables which must be stressed in order to create the
heightened tension of poetry. But it is also true that the rhythm of poetry
and the line endings cause a reader to draw out or stress syllables which
might be slurred if the passage were printed as prose. Which passage has
more monosyllables? Which has more Germanic and which more
Latinate words? These characteristics will generally apply to poetry as
opposed to prose. There will be a stress to every two or three, rather
than every four or five, syllables. There will also be more monosyllabic
and Germanic words in the poetry.

Another contrasting characteristic is what is called the **falling**

rhythm, or tendency to slack off after a stress, in prose, and the **rising rhythm,** or **lift,** in poetry. Falling rhythm is in the grain of the language, but poetry usually reverses that tendency. In the second line I have indicated stress on the second word as *HEADlights,* but, actually, both syllables are given some stress as we pronounce it. (A double stress like this is sometimes called a **hovering,** or "resolved," or "distributed" stress—as though one stress were divided between the two syllables.) Most of the lines of this poetry end in stresses, and the others have only one unaccented syllable after the stress. The term *falling rhythm* is applied to lines of poetry which end in one or more unstressed syllables—such as Longfellow's:

> By the shores of Gitche Gumee,
> By the shining Big-Sea-Water,
> Stood the wigwam of Nokomis,
> Daughter of the Moon, Nokomis.
> Dark behind it rose the forest,
> Rose the black and gloomy pine-trees,
> Rose the firs with cones upon them;
> Bright before it beat the water,
> Beat the clear and sunny water,
> Beat the shining Big-Sea-Water.

This has a strange sound in English poetry—no doubt Longfellow's attempt to catch the tom-tom rhythms he associated with the chants of Native Americans. But Whitman, too, used the music of falling rhythm, almost as a leitmotiv, or identifying melody:

> OUT of the CRAdle ENDlessly ROCKing,
> OUT of the MOCKing-bird's THROAT the MUsical SHUTtle . . .

Generally, however, poets work against the slackening effect of falling rhythm, using the natural pause of line endings to emphasize syllables and bring out stresses that might otherwise be repressed.

As the last chapter indicated, stress is peculiarly important in our language. It is therefore not surprising that the most ancient poetry in English is called *accentual* (the subject of the next chapter). Lines are measured by counting strong stresses. Accentual poetry is not the norm in modern English, though, as we shall see, a number of poets such as Hopkins and Auden have revived it, and it offers a rich source of variation of standard metrics. But to understand our most characteristic measure we must go back to the Classics—the literature of ancient Greece and Rome—and look at how that metrical system evolved through the Romance languages, reaching England with the Norman Conquest.

Classical poetry was in **quantitative meter.** Quantity refers to the length of a syllable, how long it takes to pronounce it. A line of ancient Greek or Latin poetry was measured by its number of **feet. A foot** is a unit of one or several syllables in a set pattern. For example, much Greek and Latin poetry was written in *dactylic hexameter.* **Hexameter** means six feet to the line. "Dactylic" tells us the most common kind of foot in those lines. A **dactyl** in quantitative meter is a unit consisting of a long syllable followed by two short syllables. Not all the feet in the line would be dactyls—that would be monotonous; but dactyls would predominate.

We are so accustomed to thinking in terms of stress that it may be difficult for us to understand the concept of quantity. In the ancient languages vowels could be either short or long; the long ones are marked (in modern printing) with a line over them: $\bar{a}, \bar{e}, \bar{\imath}, \bar{o}, \bar{u}.$ These vowels were sounded longer (and pronounced slightly differently) than the corresponding short vowels. A change in quantity meant a change in meaning. In Latin *fēmina* means a woman as subject of a sentence (nominative case); but *fēminā* means a woman as object of certain prepositions (ablative case), as in phrases meaning "by a woman" or "with a woman." The final *ā* is not stressed; the stress in both forms of the word is on the first syllable. To understand or speak the language one has to have an ear trained to that slight prolongation of the vowel, and the difference in quality between *FEMinuh* and *FEMinah.* A long syllable was one containing a long vowel or a short vowel followed by more than one consonant. *Fēminā,* by itself, is a dactyl. *Feminā,* by itself, is an entirely different metrical foot—an **amphimacer.** Individual words, however, do not often occur as feet. To measure feet one must look at the whole line, and syllables of one word may be combined with those of others to make up feet. If the phrase *cum fēminā* occurs in a line (meaning "with a woman"), it may be scanned (analyzed into feet) as two iambs. An **iamb** is a foot consisting of a short syllable followed by a long one: *cum FĒM\ in ā* is thus two iambs.

You will notice that we look at syllables a lot more than we do at words when we are analyzing the meter of poetry. Syllables are the units of sound a person hears—and poetry is primarily an oral art, to be spoken and heard. Words are arbitrary groupings of syllables, much more important in writing than in speaking. You say and hear something like *kmlNeer uhMINit* for what appears in print (rather artificially) as "Come in here a minute."

We have inherited from Classical poetry the convention of measuring lines of poetry by metrical feet, and have even retained the names of those feet, except that in English we have replaced the notion of quantity with that of stress. A **dactyl** in English is an accented syllable followed by two unaccented ones. An **iamb** is an unaccented one followed by an accented one. A line of **iambic pentameter**—our most common variety—is a line of five feet, predominantly iambic. If these terms confuse you, relax. I will explain them in detail in Chapter 5. For now, however, merely remember that our way of measuring lines by metrical feet and our names for the feet came from Classical poetry, though we have substituted stress for quantity. Some poets have tried writing quantitative verse in English, but the distinction between short and long syllables is much less clear, and stress cannot be suppressed, so the results tend to be more curiosities than effective poems.

Let me explain that. Suppose you work out, to your own satisfaction, which syllables are long and which syllables are short, then you compose verse with feet based on quantity, ignoring the accents. Your reader is accustomed to verse measured by stresses, and the stresses in your quantitative verse will pop up and strike the ear of the reader willy-nilly. If they are unpatterned, the writing will sound like prose. When quantitative verse works well—as it does in Robert Bridges's "Nightingales," for instance—it does so because the stress pattern happens to be satisfying, a quality irrelevant to the quantitative structure. Here are the opening lines of the poem:

> Beautiful must be the mountains whence ye come,
> And bright in the fruitful valleys the streams wherefrom
> Ye learn your song:
> Where are those starry woods? O might I wander there,
> Among the flowers, which in that heavenly air
> Bloom the year long!

Certainly there are long and short syllables—as in the dactyls *beau-ti-ful must be the moun tains whence* (the markings indicating long and short syllables). But the syllables marked long here, with a macron, are also stressed. You can see a problem with *whence.* Is it long or short? Is it stressed or not? It can be read either way, and if there were too many ambiguous syllables such as this, the poetry would disintegrate into prose (though the ambiguity works in this instance as a variation).

Let's go back to our history. As Latin broke down into the Romance languages, such as French, Italian, Spanish, Portuguese, and Rumanian, pronunciation and grammar changed. Quantity was no longer the important determinant of meaning that it had been in Latin. Lines of poetry in these languages are typically measured by the number of syllables in them. For example, a **hendecasyllabic** line, or one of eleven syllables, is common in Italian poetry. Such a measure is called **syllabic verse,** a meter based upon the number of syllables without regard to either quantity or stress.

If you listen to these languages being spoken you can understand why stress is not an important measure. Stresses occur, of course, but they are not so emphatic, and not so tied to meaning, as in English. Comedians pick up such superficial characteristics and exaggerate them for comic effect, as when one imitates a "Mexican accent" by saying hees WORDS in a singsong WAY that deesplaces the STRESS so hees language sounds FUNny. The cadence dominates. It sounds to our ears as though the song were more important than its message.

Poets still experiment with syllabic verse in English, but, as in the case of quantitative verse, their efforts tend to be foiled by the stubborn emergence of stress:

> I am writing these lines
> in syllabic verse, six
> syllables to each line,
> without regard to stress,
> to illustrate the way
> poetry is written
> in a Romance language.

Sounds like broken prose, doesn't it? You may find yourself falling into a pattern of stressing two or three syllables in each line, pushing it toward verse measured by stress. That is the nature of English erupting through the foreign form.

Good syllabic verse, like good quantitative verse in English, is likely to rely on the accidental harmonies of stress, rhyme, or other elements. One may count the syllables of the lines of Marianne Moore's "The Mind Is an Enchanted Thing" and discover that the corresponding lines in each stanza are equal. But that has little to do with the effect of the poem. Here is the first stanza:

> is an enchanted thing
>   like the glaze on a
> katydid-wing
>   subdivided by sun
>   till the nettings are legion,
> like Gieseking playing Scarlatti.

Sure enough, in each of six stanzas the first line has six syllables, the second has five, the third four, the fourth six, the fifth seven, the sixth nine. But the music of the poem is more dependent upon a da-da-DUM rhythm that comes and goes, and upon the rhymes than upon the whimsical consistency of syllable count. Her best-known poem, "Poetry," had (as originally published) five stanzas, each beginning with a nineteen-syllable line. Here are the first three lines:

> I, too, dislike it; there are things that are important beyond
>   all this fiddle.
> Reading it, however, with a perfect contempt for it, one
>   discovers in
> it, after all, a place for the genuine.

The second line has nineteen syllables, the third eleven, but in the subsequent stanzas the lines in these positions did not have the same count. The long, knobby, prosy first lines, each scrupulously counted out to have nineteen syllables, were perhaps intended to prove a point. It is a deliberately antipoetic poem, affirming, after all, the genuine. But the form indicates that the poet was writing for the eye and mind, not the ear. Maybe she counted the syllables of the first lines of the stanzas as a way of thumbing her nose at anyone who might say the poem was formless. In any case, at the end of her career, she included the poem in her collected works—cutting the final four stanzas and leaving only the three lines given on the preceding page!

Obviously there are no rules governing how lines of poetry should be measured, and if poets get some satisfaction out of counting syllables, it may not matter that readers (or, more precisely, listeners) are not likely to notice their numerical ingenuity. Many modern poets, especially, administer poetry like castor oil, giving readers what the poets think good for them, not what readers might like. That seems to me the spirit behind Marianne Moore's "Poetry." But syllabic poetry in English is at best a mental exercise, having little to do with how lines are heard.

The next two chapters will explore the two varieties of meter most common and workable in our poetry: accentual and accentual syllabic; and the chapter after that will describe the compromise between the two which characterizes much of the best modern poetry. But it is probably good for you to try for yourself and discover the strengths and weaknesses in the various ways of breaking lines which this chapter has discussed:

1. rhetorical breaks, using closed lines, perhaps with a definite cadence (especially if you use long lines). Use Whitman or the Bible as a model;
2. free verse lines using enjambment to create tension;
3. quantitative verse in which you are listening to the length rather than the stress of syllables to create patterns;
4. syllabic verse (modeled on Marianne Moore) in which you count syllables and disregard stress (and disregard rhetorical breaks).

The way to develop mastery of poetic elements is to try a wide variety of techniques. You may not settle on any of these as the technique for poems you want to save. But in the process you will have sharpened your sensitivity to some of the subtle elements of language. And it is as important to know what won't work as to know what will.

4

Listening to All God's Chillun

Accentual Meter

In northern Europe the Germanic tribes had a quite different literary tradition from that of the Greeks, Romans, and, later, the speakers of Romance languages. Their measure had nothing to do with quantitative or syllabic verse. They measured their lines by counting the number of stresses, regardless of the number of unaccented syllables. Much of their poetry had an **alliterative** formula as well, requiring the initial sounds of certain stressed syllables to be the same or similar. Old English had a rich literature in this tradition. We cannot read Old English now without special training, but the lines below illustrate the accentual and alliterative patterns of the Old English epic *Beowulf*. They open a poem I wrote about the monster in that epic, Grendel:

> Older than English: how evil emerges
> on a moor in the moonlight, emotionless, faceless,
> stiff-kneed, arms rigid, and stalks through the fog field
> until finally its fist falls, forcing the oaken door
> of whatever Heorot harbors the gentlefolk.

Read it aloud to get the flavor. It may seem clotted to you, with its pounding stresses and thick alliteration, and in this strict form (which I will explain below) the meter may not be very useful for modern poets. But they have learned a great deal from it. Some, such as Gerard Manley

Hopkins and Ezra Pound, have deliberately sought to revive it and adapt it to modern uses. It is sometimes called "native English meter," and its influence is strong in our nursery rhymes and folk poetry. You need to understand it to understand your own heritage, as well as to derive from it techniques that can be applied to your own work.

Each line is divided by a caesura. Can you find the two strong stresses in each half-line? Can you hear the alliterative pattern? The rule for this kind of poetry is that one or both of the stresses before the caesura should begin with the same sound as does the first stress after the caesura. In the second line, for instance, both *moor* and *moon* alliterate with the stressed *mo* of *emotionless*. All vowel sounds were considered to alliterate with one another in this tradition; so in the first line, both *Old* and *Eng* alliterate with the *e* of *evil* (but not with *emerges*, for the stressed syllable of that word begins with *m*). Some of the alliteration in that passage (e.g., *fog field*) is not part of the pattern but strengthens the generally alliterative texture of the verse. One can overdo this. If you try writing this form, don't get it so thick with alliteration that you become tongue-tied and unintentionally comic.

To understand accentual poetry, however, it is not the alliteration but the stresses you should attend. Listen to it in nursery rhymes:

> One, two,
> Buckle my shoe . . .

> Pease porridge hot,
> Pease porridge cold,
> Pease porridge in the pot
> Nine days old.

Do you hear how the rhythm takes over, almost forcing you into two strong stresses in each line. Sometimes sense is sacrificed. Do you say (as I do):

> PEASE porridge IN the pot

If you were reading the same words in a prose passage you would almost certainly emphasize POR and POT more than PEASE and IN, and the rhyme on POT in this verse would seem to draw some emphasis to that word. But if you read it:

> pease PORridge in the POT

it throws off the rhythm, and any child will tell you that you are saying it wrong.

Alliterative poetry is strong, vital, gutsy, but difficult to control. That is, it is difficult for the poet to manage the verse in such a way as to be sure a reader hears the same pattern of stresses the poet intended. Look at the third line of my "Grendel." There are eight syllables which can take some stress: *stiff, kneed, arms, ri, stalks, through, fog, field.* If you give more than four of them (two on each side of the caesura) a primary stress, you may lose the rhythm. That may be all right for a line here and there, as variation, but if it happens too often, the poetry will disintegrate into prose for the reader. In that line I hit *stiff, ri, stalks,* and *fog,* but you might read it differently. There is no "correct" way—and I know that, as a poet, if I let the reader's ear stray too far from mine, I will lose the music of the lines. It's the poet's job to make it work.

In that Old English verse pattern, the half-lines almost amount to independent two-beat lines. Their brevity, and the alliterative pattern, help the poet keep the lines under control. But there is a danger of monotony. A good poet will offset that by constantly varying the placement and number of unaccented syllables. (A warning which you will understand more fully after studying the next chapter: the worst thing that can happen to accentual poetry is that it comes too near to the alternating stress of accentual syllabic poetry—and thus sounds like an inept effort at the latter.)

What makes accentual (or any other) poetry interesting is variety within a set form. If the form is too loosely defined or followed, the lines read like broken prose. If they are too narrowly defined or too strictly followed, the measure becomes monotonous. Once you get those beats going in this pattern you can get variety by shifting them around in the line, doubling beats (like that "hovering" stress on *fog field*), or packing lines with strong syllables. You can't, though, in effective accentual poetry, let too many syllables go by without a strong stress. Make sure there are at least four syllables in each line which can take stresses, and not so many more than four that it is impossible to pronounce the line with only four stresses. These limits will give you plenty of room to maintain variety and surprise.

Most accentual poetry is in lines of two or three beats. Look back at the lines by Hopkins (from "The Windhover") quoted in Chapter 2. They are five-beat accentual lines. Can you find the five syllables in each that he intended to be stressed? Here is his "Pied Beauty":

> Glory be to God for dappled things—
>> For skies of couple-color as a brinded cow;
>>> For rose-moles all in stipple upon trout that swim;
>> Fresh-firecoal chestnut-falls; finches' wings;
>>> Landscapes plotted and pieced—fold, fallow, and plough;
>>> And all trades, their gear and tackle and trim.
>
> All things counter, original, spare, strange;
>> Whatever is fickle, freckled (who knows how?)
>>> With swift, slow; sweet, sour; adazzle, dim;
>> He fathers-forth whose beauty is past change:
>>> Praise Him.

How many stresses do you find in each of those lines (except the short, last one)? By now I hope your ear is tuned. If you got the rhythm of four stresses per line, you probably read the closing lines something like this:

> whatEVer is FICKle, FRECKled (who knows HOW?)
>> with SWIFT, slow; SWEET, sour; aDAZzle, DIM;
> he FATHers-forth whose BEAUty is PAST CHANGE:
>> praise HIM.

Those are, indeed, rhythmic fireworks; some strong syllables are held down under enormous pressure; others go off like rockets. The tremendous variety and energy would be lost if it were not for the regularity of the pattern, firmly established in the opening lines where the four beats are unmistakable.

For contrast, see what happens when the same poet loosens his lines into free verse. Here is the opening of "The Leaden Echo." Each new line begins at the left margin, and the indented parts are continuations of those lines.

How to keep—is there any, any, is there none such, nowhere
    known, some bow or brooch or braid or
    brace, lace, latch or catch or key to keep
Back beauty, keep it, beauty, beauty, beauty . . . from
    vanishing away?
Oh, is there no frowning of these wrinkles, ranked wrinkles deep,
Down? no waving off of these most mournful messengers, still
    messengers, sad and stealing messengers of gray?
No, there's none, there's none—oh, no, there's none!

It is still powerful writing with throbbing, explosive cadences. But with-
out the tension between the pattern of lines of set length and the pulse of
language (such as we saw in "Pied Beauty"), such lines are likely to seem
verbose, congested, squirming like a restless child with aimless energy.

Much of this discussion may be lost on you if you have difficulty hear-
ing which syllable is stressed. In speech I am sure you don't put the ac-
cent on the wrong *syl-LA-ble*. You would be unintelligible unless you
used the normal **stress** patterns of English. But many who speak in-
telligibly are confused when they try to find the stresses in language in
print. Look at a polysyllable—such as *polysyllable*. How many syllables
does it contain? Which one is stressed? Is more than one of its five sylla-
bles stressed? Which stress is primary? What happens when the word is
changed into an adjective, *polysyllabic*? Which of the following alterna-
tives are good English?

POL-y-syl-lab-ic	POL-y-syl-la-ble
pol-Y-syl-lab-ic	pol-Y-syl-la-ble
pol-y-SYL-lab-ic	pol-y-SYL-la-ble
pol-y-syl-LAB-ic	pol-y-syl-LA-ble
pol-y-syl-lab-IC	pol-y-syl-la-BLE

If you had difficulty in picking out the fourth in the list on the left and
the first in the list on the right, you need to drill yourself until you ac-
quire the skill. The dictionary will show you the preferred pronuncia-
tion. Since the marks used to indicate stress vary in different diction-
aries, check your own to see how they are marked. Notice that two

stresses are given for each of these words. In addition to the primary stresses, each has a secondary stress—on the first syllable of *polysyllabic,* on the third syllable of *polysyllable.*

Dealing with isolated words is the easy part. When you run words together in a sentence, you notice many degrees of stress, and find some stresses disappearing altogether. What syllable is accented in *apricot?* The first gets a primary stress, but the third has to have a secondary stress, or the word would sound like *APruhcut.* (All unstressed vowels in English tend to become a neutral *uh* sound, called a *schwa.*) What happens when you say *apricot pie?* You stress *pie* more heavily than *ap,* and both more than *cot*—and all three more than *ri.* If you hear those differences, you are distinguishing between primary, secondary, and tertiary stresses.

Relax. You don't have to do that to write effective poetry. But you do need to sense which syllables can and which cannot take stresses, of any degree. You learn this by listening to how the language is spoken by yourself and others.

Don't confuse stress with importance. *God* and *me* both seem like rather important words (and every monosyllabic word gets a stress when used by itself). But if you say "God help me!" you probably stress the *help* more than the other two syllables. How do you stress it? By saying it louder, longer, higher, or what? We can stress a syllable by dropping the voice as well as by raising it, by shortening as well as by lengthening a syllable. "Yes," he snapped, then, after a moment's thought, sighed, "Yes. Of course. Yes!" You probably emphasize each *yes* differently. "Does the Pope speak Latin? Yes, he does." There you probably dropped the stress on *yes* and put it on *does.*

There are no rules to guide you other than usage. You have to develop an ear for your own language in order to use it to create art. And it is interesting that there have been great authors of prose, such as Conrad and Nabokov, who wrote in a second language, or one which was not their native language, but there have been no comparable poets. It is hard enough to master the subtleties of one's native language in order to make poetry out of it. To so master a second would seem impossible!

I have been using the term *beats* in this discussion. That distinguishes the primary stresses which measure the lines of accentual meter from the whole range of stresses we will be considering in regard to accentual syllabic meter in the next chapter. In accentual syllabic poetry one must take into account all syllables which *can* bear a stress, however slight—such as the last syllable of *cleanliness,* which takes just a whisper more stress than the *i* which precedes it. On the contrary, in accentual poetry we are concerned with subduing many of the possible stresses so that the important ones, the beats, can emerge.

For example, here is a ten-syllable line by W. H. Auden which might be scanned as pentameter (a five-foot line) of accentual syllabic meter:

SIR, NO\ MAN'S EN\ em Y,\ for GIV\ ing ALL\

But if we read the whole poem (quoted below), we recognize that Auden meant it as a four-beat accentual line:

sir, NO man's ENemy, forGIVing ALL

You could not tell from that one line alone, but see if you can find the four beats in each line of the whole poem, "Petition":

Sir, no man's enemy, forgiving all
But will its negative inversion, be prodigal:
Send to us power and light, a sovereign touch
Curing the intolerable neural itch,
The exhaustion of weaning, the liar's quinsy,
And the distortions of ingrown virginity.
Prohibit sharply the rehearsed response
And gradually correct the coward's stance;
Cover in time with beams those in retreat
That, spotted, they turn though the reverse were great;
Publish each healer that in city lives
Or country houses at the end of drives;
Harrow the house of the dead; look shining at
New styles of architecture, a change of heart.

Finding those beats may have been difficult for you. By comparison, the beats of "Grendel," the poems of Hopkins, and the nursery rhymes I have quoted thump hard, often on fat monosyllables. Auden here accepts a difficult challenge, that of using accentual meter for material that is intellectual rather than emotional, reflective rather than pulsing, using a vocabulary of polysyllables and Latinate words, attempting a conversational tone. It would have been much easier to control had he used a shorter line, or used regular caesuras. But he is trying to take the meter as near prose as he can, and yet retain the structure of the four-beat line. Does it work?

It is an odd prayer, beseeching a merciful God not to show too much mercy for debilitating human weaknesses, or, at least, while he is forgiving all, to "will its negative inversion," to be prodigal in supplying correctives. The idea is difficult, the tone crisp—the opposite extreme from Hopkin's fervid raptures. These are tricky waters, and it is interesting to see how he manages to assert those beats. He avoids the regularity of alternating stress (of accentual syllabic meter), yet never lets more than three unstressed syllables go by before hitting a stress.

> COVer in TIME with BEAMS those in reTREAT
> that, SPOTted, they TURN though the reVERSE were
>   GREAT;
> PUBlish each HEALer that in CIty LIVES

In these lines, *those, though,* and *that* are all syllables which might take stresses. Is the pattern of the four beats per line strong enough to guide you past them? Does it lead you to find four syllables to stress in "And the distortions of ingrown virginity"—though the line could easily be read with only three?

Such experiments illustrate the struggle of modern poets to find a meter suited to contemporary idiom. No one talks—or ever talked—like the poetry of Beowulf, or of Hopkins, or like the accentual nursery rhymes. But we do talk, more or less, the language of "Petition." We need a medium that can accommodate intellectual language as well as emotional language, which can accommodate our polysyllables, ironic tones, subtle innuendos. This is the sort of medium Auden was trying to develop.

Unfortunately the meter of "Petition" may be too subtle for modern ears. Suppose you had read that poem elsewhere than in a chapter on accentual meter. Would you have seen any pattern at all, any way of distinguishing it from prose? This is very expert accentual meter, in which Auden was surely testing limits, moving toward a solution of the problem of how to get modern, idiomatic English into a sustaining metrical form. But he has not, here, come as near to solving that problem as he comes in other work. (In Chapter 6 we will look at another of his poems for comparison.)

You can learn something about the problems and possibilities of accentual syllabic poetry by taking a passage of prose or of free verse (yours or anyone else's) and breaking it into two- or three-beat lines. For example, here is the first strophe of Kenneth Fearing's "Resurrection" as it was published:

> You will remember the kisses, real or imagined;
> You will remember the faces that were before you, and the
>   words exchanged;
> You will remember the minute crowded with meaning, the
>   moment of pain, the aimless hour;
> You will remember the cities, and the plains, and the
>   mountains, and the sea.

I'll put it into two-beat lines:

> You will remember
> the kisses, real
> or imagined; you
> will remember the faces
> that were before you,
> and the words exchanged;
> you will remember
> the minute crowded
> with meaning, the moment
> of pain, the aimless
> hour; you
> will remember the cities,
> and the plains, and the mountains,
> and the sea, and recall . . .

(I took the last two words out of the second strophe to complete the line.) The vast, rolling, Whitmanesque sweep of Fearing's lines is reduced, chopped up; tension is increased; one dwells on individual words, listens with more attention—at the expense of losing the coherence of mounting cadences and parallel structure. I am not suggesting that Fearing's poem is improved by rewriting it in accentual meter, but you can see by this process some of the advantages and disadvantages. The enjambments jerk and surprise. Some phrases linger on the ear. We see effects (such as the alliteration of the phrase "with meaning, the moment") which we might miss in the longer line. That little line, "hour; you," demanding a beat on each word, seems to me a haunting variation on lines that ripple with syllables such as, "and the plains, and the mountains." Fearing's poetry seems to me too loose and prosaic, too rambling. He might have strengthened it with a tighter metrical structure. But, of course, the poems would not have come out the same. When you write in a two-beat line (or a three-beat line), you shape each line as you go along for maximum effectiveness and variation, which is quite another matter than arbitrarily breaking up long lines into short ones.

But two- and three-beat lines are too limited for many poetic purposes—and, as I have said, longer accentual lines tend to be intractable. We need a more flexible medium if we want a meter that is suitable for the whole range of material we want to deal with as poets. Understanding that, we can see the importance of the emergence of accentual syllabic meter as the norm in our language.

5

Lisping in Numbers

Accentual Syllabic Meter

In discussing accentual meter we were concerned with only those primary stresses which dominate phrases, the ones we call beats. In ordinary prose or spoken English, as in accentual meter, many stresses on individual words are swallowed up in phrases. For example, when you read this sentence quickly, which syllables do you stress?

> All the time she was talking about cleanliness she was indifferently flicking her cigaret on the rug.

You might read it somewhat differently, but I put the first strong stress on *talk,* then on *clean, flick, cig, rug. Dif* gets a slight stress, too, or one would have to race through eight or nine unaccented syllables in a row, which is almost impossible to do. (Eight or nine depending on whether you say *fernt* or *fer-ent,* either of which is acceptable.) But look what happens to that word when it is put into verse:

> She talked of cleanliness while she
> was flicking her ash indifferently.

Can you find four stresses in each of those lines? Notice that both *ness* and *ly* are raised into prominence by the rhythm of the lines, though your dictionary will indicate there is not even a secondary stress on either syllable. Reading the lines aloud you should not, of course, exaggerate by making those syllables as strong in stress as *talked, flick,* and *ash.* But the verse form invites you to dwell a little on them, to savor more of the richness of the words.

We are now far from the swashbuckling slam-bang stresses of *Beowulf.* These lines are in accentual syllabic meter, and though you might not know the names of the feet or how to scan them, you know how to read them from your long familiarity with the conventions. The difference between the way we read verse such as this and the way we read Auden's "Petition" (quoted in the last chapter) is that our attention has shifted from subduing stresses to feeling out which syllables *can* take a bit of stress.

Some syllables cannot. For instance, you know the *bows* in *elbows* cannot take a stress without distorting the language. That sometimes happens in amateur verse, or, especially, in folk ballads in which a tune can cover a multitude of metrical abominations. The modern American poet John Crowe Ransom was having fun with folk ballads when he wrote of his "Captain Carpenter":

> Their strokes and counters whistled in the wind
> I wish he had delivered half his blows
> But where she should have made off like a hind
> The bitch bit off his arms at the elbows.

Both rhymes *(wind/hind* and *blows/elbows)* are deliberately wrenched for comic effect, the first being an eye rhyme, the second a displacement of stress.

When two streams flow together there is a muddying of the waters. Old English had many short words with strong beats; accentual poetry was excellently adapted to its grain. After the Norman Conquest the language began to absorb polysyllabic words that had fewer stresses. For three hundred years English poetry was in a turmoil, until, in the latter part of the fourteenth century, Chaucer (and other influential poets, such as John Gower) achieved a combination of accentual and syllabic metrics which still characterizes most of the poetry in our language. It was another hundred years before, in the work of Wyatt, Surrey, Spenser, Marlowe, Shakespeare, and dozens of other poets of the Renaissance, the metrical discoveries of Chaucer came into full flower and English poetry truly found its tongue.

We can almost read the poetry of Chaucer without special study, though we might not hear its delicate music because pronunciation has changed. Here is a little of Chaucer's poetry (in a slightly modernized form), from his description of the Squire in the Prologue to the *Canterbury Tales:*

> Synging he was, or floytinge, al the day;
> He was as fressh as is the month of May.
> Short was his gowne, with sleves longe and wyde.
> Wel koude he sit on hors and faire ryde;
> He koude songes make and wel endite,
> Juste and eek daunce, and well purtreye and write.
> So hote he lovede that by nightertale
> He slepte namoor than dooth a nightyngale.
> Curteis he was, lowely, and servysable,
> And carf biforn his fader at the table.

You might enjoy trying to pronounce that. Each consonant is sounded. For instance, *nightertale,* which means "nighttime," comes out something like NEEKT-er-TAHL. The *s* is soft—a hiss, not a *z*. Vowels have their "continental" values: *a, e, i, o, u* are *ah, ay, ee, oh, oo.* Here is a rough approximation of the sounds of the first few lines:

> SEEN-geeng hay WASS, ohr FLOI-ting, AHL thay
>   DAHEE;
> hay WASS ahs FRAYSH ahs EES thay MOANTH ohf
>   MAYEE.
> SHORT wass hees GOON, weeth SLAY-vays LOHNG ahnd
>   WEED.
> wayl KOWD hay SEET on HORS ahnd FAYR-uh REED.
> hay KOWD-uh SOHN-gus MAHK ahnd WAYL ayn-DEET. . . .

Notice the different pronunciations of *koude* in the last two lines Final *e, es,* and *ed* were sometimes sounded and sometimes not, according to complex rules. Your best guide is to pronounce them or not as the rhythm requires. I have exaggerated the rhythm in this passage so you could see it; in ordinary reading one would stress many of those syllables lightly or not at all:

he was as FRESH as is the MONTH of MAY

Was and *is* can take stresses, so the verse moves along smoothly in its generally alternating rhythm. Some lines start with a stress, or a reversed first foot (DUM-da), but otherwise the meter is regular. Here is how Nevil Coghill rendered the lines into modern English:

> Singing he was, or fluting all the day;
> He was as fresh as is the month of May.
> Short was his gown, the sleeves were long and wide;
> He knew the way to sit a horse and ride.
> He could make songs and poems and recite,
> Knew how to joust and dance, to draw and write.
> He loved so hotly that till dawn grew pale
> He slept as little as a nightingale.
> Courteous he was, lowly and serviceable,
> And carved to serve his father at the table.

The stress has moved forward on *serviceable*. Chaucer would have said something like SAIR-vee-SAH-bul, with the primary stress on the SAH, giving a smoother reading than the modern word with its primary stress on the first syllable and only the slightest stress, if any, on the third, making an awkward thyme with *at the table*.

Typically Chaucer's lines are **decasyllabic** or **hendecasyllabic**—each has ten syllables, or eleven if the last is unaccented—following the model of French and other continental poetry. But he combined regularity of syllable count with a general regularity of accent, alternating unstressed and stressed syllables. The decasyllabic frame held the verse firm even when the stresses went slack, so he did not have to maintain the insistent stress of accentual verse.

The result is a more delicate, variable music, allowing polysyllabic words and words of relatively light stress to flow into place smoothly. Many lines can be read with only three or four stresses, yet the verse doesn't limp. This meter could accommodate the burgeoning vocabulary of English, especially the infusion of French polysyllables, in ways that accentual meter could not.

The blend of syllabic and accentual meters which emerged with Chaucer and his contemporaries has come to be called by the awkward label *accentual syllabic.* These lines of Chaucer's have substantially the same measure that characterizes the work of Shakespeare, Milton, Dryden, Pope, Wordsworth, Keats, Browning, Yeats, Frost—indeed, of all the major poets in the language. A tradition persists in a culture because it expresses something natural and essential, something deep in the grain. Poets have not been writing iambic pentameter for seven centuries because they were conformists or lacked imagination. They used that verse medium for the same reason that a fine furniture maker is likely to prefer to work with wood. It suits the need for flexibility, strength, beauty, elegance, dignity, weight, and other aesthetic and practical considerations. Of course most poets experiment with alternatives, too, and, especially in our own century in America, many have found the "iambic yoke" a burden, as though the metrical form itself were responsible for what they felt to be the monotony and conformity of the poetry of their elders. There are, indeed, limitations and artificialities inherent in a strict accentual syllabic meter, as will be discussed in Chapter 6. But it is interesting that many who throw off the yoke of this form of metrics do not replace it with any other measure. They cast off meter altogether and write free verse.

The terms borrowed from the Classics, such as *iambic* and *pentameter,* or even *accentual syllabic,* have not been known by, or used by, most of the poets writing in this meter. I use such terms because they make it easier to talk about verse techniques, just as it is easier to talk about automobile mechanics if you use terms such as carburetor, gasket, and piston.

The terms of **prosody,** or the science of metrics, have been applied by people analyzing what poets have practiced. It is obvious from their work that Shakespeare and Milton and all the other great poets were sensitive to the phenomena these terms refer to because they were consistent in their use of certain techniques. But they probably did not know or use the terms in everyday composition.

Many early poets did not use the term *metrics,* but instead *numbers,* as when Alexander Pope wrote:

> As yet a child, nor yet a fool to fame,
> I lisped in numbers, for the numbers came.

For him, as for Chaucer, the standard line in English was decasyllabic, or made up of ten syllables. And these syllables generally had an alternating stress: *da DUM da DUM da DUM da DUM da DUM.* Suppose you had a word at the end with one or more unstressed syllables after that last DUM—giving you *da DUM da,* or *da DUM da da,* and making a line of eleven or twelve syllables. That was acceptable to Chaucer, and to later poets. Prosodists call such syllables **hypermetrical,** meaning the syllables don't count in analyzing the meter. Suppose that, for variety, you started with an accent, keeping ten syllables. The line would then begin *DUM da da DUM da DUM.* That, too, was an acceptable variation. Suppose that, now and again, an extra unstressed syllable crept in, giving us *da DUM da da DUM da DUM,* again making the line have more than ten syllables. That, too, was all right.

Another source of variety results from the various degrees of intensity of stress. What happens to the word *of* in these two phrases: "the bottom of my heart" and "she was warm of heart"? In the first it may take a little stress; in the second it is unstressed. Such ambiguity permitted a great deal of flexibility, and relief from monotony, in alternating rhythm. Suppose you were to displace an accent—having two unstressed, then two stressed syllables: "of the night wind." That was acceptable.

And that was about all. Believe it or not, I have just told you the few variations which account for about 90 of those you find in metrical verse in English. Let's review them:

1 DUM da da DUM da DUM
2 da da DUM DUM da DUM
3 da DUM da da DUM da DUM
4 da DUM da DUM da DUM da

Instead of worrying about the number of syllables in each line, it is simpler to think of units, or **feet.** The basic unit is *da DUM*—an **iamb.** In line 1, one unit is reversed—giving us *DUM da*—a **trochee**. In the second line, a stress has been displaced, moved from one unit to the next, giving us a unit without a stress, *da da*—a **pyrrhic**—and another with two stresses, *DUM DUM*—a **spondee**. In the third line, an extra unstressed syllable gives us a trisyllabic unit, *da da DUM*—an **anapest**. In line 4, there is an extra, or hypermetrical, syllable at the end of the line, which doesn't fit into any of the units.

A few other variations sometimes occur, and names of other feet such as **dactyl** *(DUM da da)* and **amphibrach** *(da DUM da)* are sometimes used to describe them. But most of what you need to know to **scan** (that is, to analyze the meter of) poetry in English—or to write it—depends upon a thorough understanding of the few feet named in the last paragraph: iamb, trochee, anapest, pyrrhic, spondee (and upon your not being confused by hypermetrical syllables). At first this may make verse seem very limited. Why merely these variations, and almost no others? The answer is not that poets were following rules. They were, as artists, concerned only with writing what would be satisfying and effective. If there is too much regularity, the rhythm becomes dull. If there is too much variety, the poetic texture disintegrates—you have prose. They found out what would work. The terms are merely labels for what they found.

Let me now fill in words to correspond to the syllables in my *da DUM* lines. Compare these lines carefully with those on the preceding page:

1 Whispering branches scrape
2 on the cold panes of thought.
3 I dream of escape, but I
4 am caught by inner whispers.

First notice that you are concerned with syllables, not words. (And the syllables do not necessarily correspond to the syllabification indicated in the dictionary, which is a convenience for printers. Your concern is with the syllables as you actually pronounce them.) *WHIS per* is a trochee, *ing BRANCH* an iamb. Notice, also, that any two readers might, in some places, stress different syllables. Do you stress both *I* and *DREAM* in line 3, or do you read it as *i DREAM,* an iamb? Do you stress both of the first two syllables of line 4, or only the second? I meant those both as iambs, but you might read them as spondees, and it doesn't matter. A spondee works anywhere as a substitute for an iamb.

As you analyze those lines into feet you are learning **scansion.** In my early years as a poet I scanned thousands of lines by dozens of poets of various periods, learning most from Shakespeare and Frost. One scans to learn what works—what makes some lines haunting, moving, powerful, why some hobble. Recently I encountered an inept effort at the first two lines of a **limerick:**

> There once was a stupendous poet
> Who was good but did not know it.

Do these lines pain your ears as they do mine? Would scansion help us see what went wrong? Whether you have ever analyzed one metrically or not, you probably have the rhythm of a limerick in your head:

> There was an old man of the Dee
> Who was sadly annoyed by a Flea;
> When he said, "I will scratch it,"
> They gave him a hatchet,
> Which grieved that Old Man of the Dee.

As in this example, by Edward Lear, one expects three stresses in each of the first two lines. The rhythm is generally anapestic—*da da DUM da da DUM,* though anapestic lines easily absorb occasional iambs as variations. How do you read those two lines I have called inept? Do you stress the *ONCE* or the *WAS?* Either is possible, but I would automatically stress the *ONCE.* The limerick pattern then makes me want to say:

> There ONCE \ was a STU \ pen dous PO \ et

Which requires a mispronunciation of *stupendous.* The meter is simply out of control. In the second line there are too many words which can take stresses but needn't be stressed. One doesn't know how to read it, but a limerick reading would make it at best awkward and unnatural:

> who was GOOD \ but DID \ not KNOW \ it

Minor revisions would improve the meter considerably:

> There was once a stupendous poet
> Who was good, but he sure didn't know it.

Not great, but better. Does your ear tell you the difference? It involves moving the *ONCE* to a position where it can take up the slack in the first line, and inserting a syllable, *SURE,* which takes a definite stress in the second. If you scanned the original, you would see the problem clearly. Most people would probably stress the *ONCE* and not stress *DID,* so you get:

> there ONCE \ was a \ stu PEN \ dous PO \ et
> who was GOOD \ but did \ not KNOW \ it

That makes four feet instead of three in the first line, and, in both lines, a pyrrhic before an iamb, leaving three unstressed syllables in a row—a wobbly passage for comic verse. (Comic verse generally requires technical polish in order to be funny. It may, like a clown on a slack wire, seem to be clumsy, but the audience has to be sure that the clumsiness is part of the act, not the result of ineptitude.)

Perfectly regular verse, on the other hand, would be as monotonous as a metronome. The ideal is not regularity but appropriateness: how the meter relates to what you are saying. In his "An Essay on Criticism," Pope illustrates this principle beautifully:

1 True ease in writing comes from art, not chance,
2 As those move easiest who have learn'd to dance.
3 'Tis not enough no harshness gives offence,
4 The sound must seem an Echo to the sense:
5 Soft is the strain when Zephyr gently blows,
6 And the smooth stream in smoother numbers flows;
7 But when loud surges lash the sounding shoar,
8 The hoarse, rough verse should like the torrent roar:
9 When Ajax strives some rock's vast weight to throw,
10 The line too labours, and the words move slow;
11 Not so, when swift Camilla scours the plain,
12 Flies o'er th' unbending corn, and skims along the main.

Let's look at some of the effects in detail. Line 5 starts with a trochee followed by an iamb, *DUM da da DUM*, a common beginning for an iambic line. The phrase is unified by the alliteration of the stressed syllables, making it softly whisper. The sixth line begins with that combination of a pyrrhic and a spondee we have mentioned, *da da DUM DUM* (sometimes called an **Ionic** after a four-syllable foot in Classical poetry: // ∪∪ or ∪∪ //). Again alliteration helps unify the phrase. The seventh line is more irregular. The beginning iamb is followed by a spondee, throwing three stresses together, *da DUM DUM DUM,* and the line rocks appropriately to its content. The same device starts the eighth line, with even longer syllables and rougher sounds. And *SHOULD* in that line also requires a stress. How about *LIKE*? You may stress it or not: the foot "should like" may be read either as a spondee or a trochee, but, in either case, it is an unusual variation, especially coming so late in the line. (Notice that most of Pope's variations occur at the beginnings of lines, then the meter smooths out to reestablish the norm.) Four or five stresses thus pile up like the storm itself. In these lines stresses are used to suggest the violence of the action, and in the ninth a similar pile-up of an iamb and two spondees in the middle of the line is used to convey a sense of laborious effort and weight with five successive stresses, all on long syllables with emphatic consonants. That passage is summarized in the tenth line, where the combination of iamb and spondee is used twice—at the beginning and at the end of the line—balancing and closing off the couplet and the idea. Now Pope moves to the other extreme. He gets speed and lightness in the eleventh and twelfth lines by using short syllables and quick anapests. Line 11 is metrically regular, but slithers with *s*'s and *l*'s. Line 12 starts with a trochee followed by an anapest, which throws three unaccented syllables together, quite a radical irregularity for Pope. The tongue races.

These little variations seem simple, but they have a critical effect on the sound of the verse. Listen again to the differences in rhythm in these line openings:

> Soft is the strain
> And the smooth stream
> But when loud surges
> The hoarse, rough verse
> The line too labours
> Flies o'er th' unbending corn

They would have little effect, of course, were it not for the prevailing regularity of the meter. In order to have variation, you have to have something to vary.

Did you notice that line 12 has six feet? A line of **hexameter,** called an **Alexandrine,** sometimes occurs as a variation on **pentameter** (or lines of five feet). Pope had made fun of this practice a little earlier in this same poem:

> A needless Alexandrine ends the song,
> That, like a wounded snake, drags its slow length along.

In the line that tells how Camilla flies he compensates for the length of the line with the swiftness and lightness of the syllables. In the Alexandrine about the snake he deliberately stretches it out with a couple of spondees, using the meter to make it tedious. The whole of "An Essay on Criticism" is an exercise in virtuosity by the young man (it was published when Pope was twenty-two) who lisped in numbers and now was ready to instruct the world on how to write poetry.

Before leaving this passage, let's look at some of the lightly stressed and unstressed syllables. In the second line, "As those move easiest who have learned to dance," the third foot is an anapest, forcing a slight stress on *WHO*. In the fourth line, "an Echo to the sense," a slight stress may be heard on *TO*. That foot (*o to*) could be read either as a pyrrhic or an iamb. In the tenth line, "The line too labours, and the words move slow," a light stress may be heard on *AND*—or the foot could be read as a pyrrhic *(bours, and)*. In each of these cases the final syllable of the foot could be said to have a **theoretical accent** meaning that the syllable *can* take some stress, though it might not be stressed in normal reading. For contrast, look at *And the* in the sixth line. *AND* might be stressed, making the foot a trochee instead of a pyrrhic, but *the* cannot be stressed at all.

This distinction might seem fussy, but it is helpful in understanding why the poetry of Pope seems so smooth and regular (tiresomely so to many readers), and why that of other poets can seem much more ragged and tense, even when they are using the same basic meter. About eighty percent of the feet in Pope's poetry (or four out of five) are iambs, and many of the pyrrhics (such as those we have looked at) can be read as iambs with theoretical stresses. Another factor is the way he used **caesuras,** the natural pauses. Pope's lines tend to be balanced and closed:

> The sound must seem//an Echo to the sense:
> Soft is the strain//when Zephyr gently blows,
> And the smooth stream//in smoother numbers flows.

The first half balances with the second, and the caesura tends to fall right in the middle of the line or not far off-center.

As you move from understanding accentual verse to understanding accentual syllabic verse you have to shift gears just as poets did in the fourteenth century. Instead of listening for those emphatic beats, you concentrate on the rather mysterious units called feet. They are mysterious because they seem so arbitrary. Sometimes, as in the spondee *(DUM DUM)* or **amphimacer** *(DUM da DUM),* they have two stresses. (Indeed, the Greeks recognized one with three, the **molussus,** the English equivalent of which would be *DUM DUM DUM,* "dark wet night.") On the other hand, there can be feet with no stress at all: pyrrhics *(da da).* (And, sure enough, the Greeks had a word for a three-syllable foot without stress, the **tribrach,** *da da da,* which could be applied to "ing a dis" in a line such as "While feeling a discomfort he lay still.") It compounds frustration, if not confusion, to realize that neither Chaucer nor most of the poets who followed him up to modern times ever actually analyzed verse this way. They just wrote it, with rather amazing metrical consistency, and these complicated adaptations of Classical metrical terms have been introduced by prosodists to explain the phenomena of the poets' practice. Can a poet today simply ignore the whole tangle?

Yes and no. Yes, because so many do. No, because (unless they have remarkably sharp ears and have picked up the techniques intuitively, without learning the terminology) they would write much better poetry if they understood how accentual syllabic meter works. Essentially the problem of poets today is the same as it was for Chaucer: how to accommodate all those Latinate polysyllables which are so essential to our language and thought.

Try writing a dozen lines on a serious subject without using Latinate polysyllables, and you will understand the need to which accentual syllabic meter was a response. In the last chapter, analyzing "Petition," we saw Auden wrestling with the problem, using accentual meter. The result was rather prosaic—a rhythm probably lost on most ears. How can we make music out of that language?

Recently I have been watching the plays of Shakespeare in excellent public television productions, and I was struck again by the flood of polysyllables, by the way Shakespeare could make music out of the most intractable material. Forget about the great passages for a moment and consider an undistinguished one. King Henry V is asking the Archbishop of Canterbury whether he has a right to claim the French throne:

> My learned lord, we pray you to proceed,
> And justly and religiously unfold
> Why the law Salique, that they have in France,
> Or should, or should not, bar us in our claim:
> And God forbid, my dear and faithful lord,
> That you should fashion, wrest, or bow your reading,
> Or nicely charge your understanding soul
> With opening titles miscreate, whose right
> Suits not in native colours with the truth;
> For God doth know how many, now in health,
> Shall drop their blood in approbation
> Of what your reverence shall incite us to.
> Therefore take heed how you impawn our person,
> How you awake the sleeping sword of war:
> We charge you, in the name of God, take heed;
> For never two such kingdoms did contend
> Without much fall of blood; whose guiltless drops
> Are every one a woe, a sore complaint
> 'Gainst him whose wrongs give edge unto the swords
> That make such waste in brief mortality.
> Under this conjuration, speak, my lord;
> For we will hear, note, and believe in heart
> That what you speak is in your conscience washt
> As pure as sin with baptism.

To write thousands upon thousands of such lines the poet had to have some easy technique, ready at hand, flexible enough to deal with any subject, strong enough to maintain a high pitch of poetry. You should be able to scan the passage now. The first line is perfectly regular, the kind of line a poet needs every so often to establish the key, the norm. The second requires one of those pyrrhics (or, if you prefer, a theoretical stress on *ly*). The third line is rough:

> WHY the \ LAW sal \ LIQUE, that \ they HAVE \
> in FRANCE \

Three trochees in a row, then a little skip, such as a soldier takes who finds himself out of step, to get back on the iambic track. Can you do the fourth? Do you find the mid-line spondee followed by a pyrrhic, underscoring the dramatic emphasis? The fifth line reasserts the norm, as do the sixth and seventh. How about the eighth?

With opening titles miscreate, whose right

I would guess an actor would slur the last two syllables of *opening* into one, or you could read *en ing TI* as an anapest. It doesn't matter. *Miscreate* is archaic, but its meaning is obvious, and because its position tells us it's an adjective, we know to stress the first syllable and read the last two as a pyrrhic. After a couple of regular lines we have:

Shall drop their blood in approbation

Can you find the five feet here? It is from such evidence that we know that in Shakespeare's time the *tion* ending was (at least sometimes) pronounced as two syllables:

AP pro BA ti on

probably with a slight stress on the *on* (and the *t* pronounced like *s*). Similarly, nine lines below, the *ty* of *mortality* takes a bit more stress than the *i* that precedes it. (You may scan such feet as pyrrhics or iambs: it doesn't matter.) Otherwise the lines are regular, with such common variations (e.g., a reversed first foot, an occasional spondee) as we have discussed.

This book cannot teach you to write great poetry: that's up to you. But it can help you write competent poetry, and there is no greatness without at least minimal competence. Shakespeare's contemporaries, many of them excellent dramatists and moving poets, lacked his greatness. But perhaps even more critically, they lacked his competence—precisely in such relatively neutral passages as the one quoted above. They did not have the mastery of meter to get through such necessary material with sustained dramatic power and music. Ponder those pyrrhics, those theoretical accents. They may liberate your tongue.

I have dwelt on iambic pentameter and its variations because it has for seven centuries been the norm of English poetry, but you should try your hand at other lengths of lines than pentameter and experiment with other feet than iambs. A one-foot line is called **monometer,** and those of two, three, and so on to eight are called **dimeter, trimeter, tetrameter, pentameter, hexameter, septameter, octameter.** You probably know by heart at least one line of trochaic octameter:

> Once upon a midnight dreary, while I pondered, weak and
>   weary

That, of course, is the opening of Edgar Allan Poe's "The Raven." The internal rhyme *(dreary/weary)* points up the fact that it breaks into two lines of tetrameter, as octameter lines tend to do. You may also know some familiar lines of anapestic tetrameter:

> Have you heard of the wonderful one-hoss shay
> That was built in such a logical way
> It ran a hundred years to a day,
> And then, of a sudden, it—ah, but stay,
> I'll tell you what happened without delay,
> Scaring the parson into fits,
> Frightening people out of their wits,—
> Have you ever heard of that, I say?

That is the first verse paragraph of Oliver Wendell Holmes's "The Deacon's Masterpiece." Scan it to see what variations work in this meter. For example, how do you account for the sixth and seventh lines?

> SCAR ing the PAR son IN to FITS,
> FRIGHT en ing PEO ple OUT of their WITS—

Something is obviously missing. Since the basic meter of the poem is anapestic (with frequent iambs as substitutions), we have to assume that the first feet of these lines are **monosyllabic,** the unstressed syllables being dropped from their beginnings.

Here is a stanza from the same poet's "The Last Leaf":

> But now his nose is thin,
> And it rests upon his chin
>   Like a staff,
> And a crook is in his back,
> And a melancholy crack
>   In his laugh.

The **scheme** of such a stanza can be given as a formula, with figures for the number of feet per line and letters to indicate which lines rhyme with which: $a^3 a^3 b^2 c^3 c^3 b^2$. The formula tells us the first two lines rhyme and are trimeter, the third rhymes with the last and is dimeter, and so on. The dimeter lines, consistently throughout the poem, begin with monosyllabic feet. Such lines are sometimes called **headless.** Headless lines are often used in songs, such as Shakespeare's:

> Fear no more the heat o' the sun,
>> Nor the furious winter's rages;
> Thou thy worldly task hast done,
>> Home art gone, and ta'en thy wages.
> Golden lads and girls all must,
> As chimney-sweepers, come to dust.

Since all lines are the same length (in spite of the arbitrary indentations), the stanza could be described as tetrameter *a b a b c c*. The anapests in the first and second lines should probably be read as iambs. The omission of the *f* implies that *o' the* should somehow be pronounced as one unaccented syllable. And *FUR yus* is a passable pronunciation of *furious*. (Incidentally, the contractions older poets used to keep their meter even—such as *o'* and *ta'en*—are now considered archaic; a modern poet would simply put in the extra syllable and count an anapest in the scansion.)

Lines shorter than four feet or longer than six are uncommon in our poetry. They may be used for special effects—for example, in stanzas that have a pattern of lines of various lengths. Tetrameter is sometimes called **dogtrot:** it's a quick, easy meter, very suitable for folksy narratives, songs, poems that need to trot right along. But tetrameter can be moving, too. You may be familiar with Andrew Marvell's "To His Coy Mistress," which shifts from an apparently light tone, a witty string of hyperboles (or exaggerations) to make fun of the idea of timeless love, into a more serious passage:

> But at my back I alwaies hear
> Times wingèd Charriot hurrying near:
> And yonder all before us lye
> Deserts of vast Eternity.
> Thy Beauty shall no more be found;
> Nor, in thy marble Vault, shall sound
> My ecchoing Song: then Worms shall try
> That long preserv'd Virginity:
> And your quaint Honour turn to dust;
> And into ashes all my Lust.
> The Grave's a fine and private place,
> But none I think do there embrace.

What effect have the anapests in the second line?

> TIME'S WING \ ed CHAR \ ri ot HUR \ ry ing NEAR \

Do you notice the resonance of the two enjambments followed by eye rhymes: *lye/Eternity, try/Virginity*? What effect on the movement of the poem has that strong caesura after "Song"? If you look at the whole poem you will see that the first verse paragraph has a relatively lighthearted, teasing tone, compared to the second (quoted above). How would you describe the tone of the last couplet above? Contrast it with the opening of the third (and final) verse paragraph:

> Now therefore, while the youthful hew
> Sits on thy skin like morning dew,
> And while thy willing Soul transpires
> At every pore with instant Fires,
> Now let us sport us while we may;

You can see that these tetrameter couplets, most of them closed, have something like the flexibility we have noticed in pentameter, yet the swift pace of the meter has a very different emotional effect from pentameter lines.

At another extreme are lines of dactylic hexameter, from Longfellow's "Prelude to Evangeline":

> This is the forest primeval. The murmuring pines and hemlocks,
> Bearded with moss, and in garments green, indistinct in the
>   twilight,
> Stand like druids of eld, with voices sad and prophetic,
> Stand like harpers hoar, with beards that rest on their bosoms.

It would be a good exercise for you to scan this passage to familiarize yourself with **falling meter** (that is, meter with feet trailing off in unaccented syllables). The opening establishes the measure:

> THIS is the\ FOR est pri\ ME val. the\ . . .

What is the last foot of each of the above lines? Do you find this variation elsewhere in the lines? Anapests and spondees (both of which end in stresses) are frequent variants in iambic poetry, or **rising meter.** Similarly, falling feet (trochees and dactyls) can be easily interchanged for one another in falling meter. Trochees must be used with care as variants in iambic verse. They are common, as we have seen, at the beginnings of lines and after caesuras, but tend to disrupt the meter when used elsewhere. Dactyls almost never occur in iambic verse. And iambs and anapests almost never occur in trochaic or dactylic verse. Spondees sometimes do, as they can fit into a rising or falling pattern.

By careful management of caesuras, Longfellow is able to keep his lines above from breaking in two, but Alexandrines, or hexameter lines, have a tendency to break down into two trimeter halves, as do all lines longer than pentameter. We saw that in the octameter passage from Poe's "The Raven." Septameter (sometimes called "old fourteener" for its fourteen syllables) tends to break into lines of tetrameter and trimeter, the pattern of the ballad stanza. For example, one might take a septameter couplet:

> There lived a wife at Usher's Well, and a wealthy wife was she;
> She had three stout and stalwart sons, and sent them o'er the sea.

and break them into a ballad stanza:

There lived a wife at Usher's Well,
  And a wealthy wife was she;
She had three stout and stalwart sons,
  And sent them o'er the sea.

A small x is used in the formula for lines that don't rhyme: $x^4 a^3 x^4 a^3$. Some poems in English have been written in hexameter, but it is an unwieldly line, difficult to read in one breath, with a strong tendency to dissolve into trimeter. As I have mentioned, Alexandrines, or hexameter lines, occur most commonly as variations in pentameter poems.

It is the asymmetry of the pentameter line which makes it so effective, especially for longer poems. It doesn't break down. It can have continuously varying subunits, created by moving the caesuras around, or it can roll out its full length without a pause. It can achieve great dignity and eloquence or be adapted to the raucous fits and starts of comedy; can convey meditation, argument, reasoning, lyrical grace, or wild passion. There are good reasons why so many poets have settled on it for their major work, reasons which you can discover best by practice. Experiment with other accentual syllabic meters and line lengths so that you learn both their strengths and limitations. I think you will learn in the process why iambic pentameter has such a strong hold on the poetry of our language.

6

Getting the Beat

Modern Adaptations of Accentual Syllabic Meter

I hope those pyrrhics and theoretical stresses are still bothering you. On the one hand they draw out the sounds of syllables we might slur over, making us hear a music in the language which would otherwise be lost. On the other hand they are undeniably artificial, making the reading of poetry quaint or strained for many. Modern poets have generally sought greater naturalness of expression, a looser way of dealing with the unaccented syllables in polysyllabic words and with the little business words that pepper our speech. Pyrrhics, or, especially, the theoretical stresses on syllables such as the *ty* in *mortality*, have been a major obstacle.

It is interesting to see the efforts of a young poet in the early years of this century to deal with the problem. In Robert Frost's first book, published in 1913, two poems appear on facing pages. There is no reason to believe that they were written one after the other, but they are carefully arranged as a contrast. One of the pervasive themes of the book, *A Boy's Will,* is Frost's leaving behind an immature desire to escape the world and moving toward mature involvement with and acceptance of it. Most of the poems had a gloss by the author in the table of contents. For "The Vantage Point" he wrote, *"And again scornful, but there is no one hurt."* Here is the poem:

> If tired of trees I seek again mankind,
>> Well I know where to hie me—in the dawn,
>> To a slope where the cattle keep the lawn,
> There amid lolling juniper reclined,
> Myself unseen, I see in white defined
>> Far off the homes of men, and farther still,
>> The graves of men on an opposing hill,
> Living or dead, whichever are to mind.
>
> And if by noon I have too much of these,
>> I have but to turn on my arm, and lo,
>> The sunburned hillside sets my face aglow,
> My breathing shakes the bluet like a breeze,
>> I smell the earth, I smell the bruisèd plant,
>> I look into the crater of the ant.

He has been wandering in the woods all night, escaping people. If he wants people he can lie on the hill and look down upon them. If he gets tired of them again he can return his attention to nature—indeed, look *down* upon it, finding a wry and condescending analogy between an anthill and a human settlement. He is aloof, uninvolved, has a lot of leisure, feels rather superior, very sensitive and delicate. He doesn't go—he hies himself. Cattle don't graze in a pasture—they keep the lawn. He doesn't lie down—he reclines; not on the juniper—but amid it. He doesn't think of things but has them to mind. Now I doubt that Frost or anyone else speaking English in that era used words such as *hie* and *amid* and *lo* and *keep* (in the sense used here) in conversation. These are literary borrowings, like the pirouette "Myself unseen, I see. . ." He is letting the reader know he is a well-read young man. When he writes poetry he makes it poetic—which means he makes it sound like poetry he has read. I don't know whether Frost was adolescent when he wrote this, but these are adolescent attitudes. One can find them banging and brooding around the house any day of the week.

On the facing page is "Mowing," which Frost glossed, *"He takes up life simply with the small tasks"*:

There was never a sound beside the wood but one,
And that was my long scythe whispering to the ground.
What was it it whispered? I knew not well myself;
Perhaps it was something about the heat of the sun,
Something, perhaps, about the lack of sound—
And that was why it whispered and did not speak.
It was no dream of the gift of idle hours,
Or easy gold at the hand of fay or elf:
Anything more than the truth would have seemed too weak
To the earnest love that laid the swale in rows,
Not without feeble-pointed spikes of flowers
(Pale orchises), and scared a bright green snake.
The fact is the sweetest dream that labor knows.
My long scythe whispered and left the hay to make.

This poem is about work, about loving work—an attitude decidedly not adolescent. It is in the past tense, whereas "The Vantage Point" is in the present. "Mowing" remembers and reflects on experience; "The Vantage Point" says, "This is the kind of person *I am*." There are still some phony, literary touches in "Mowing" (for example, "I knew not well myself"), but these are faintly satirical, dismissing fantasy as precisely the music he was *not* hearing:

It was no dream of the gift of idle hours,
Or easy gold at the hand of fay or elf.

Change "no" to "a" and these lines might appear in "The Vantage Point." They even seem to fit by their length on the page. But both leisure and fantasy are rejected in the poem. The poet has rolled up his sleeves to get to serious business. By the time Frost collected his poems for his first volume he was able to look back upon his immature poems and attitudes with ironic amusement, to place them cheek by jowl with more mature work so we would not fail to see his growth.

What has all this to do with pesky pyrrhics? Scan the poems and find out. For example, the two lines last quoted would not fit metrically into "The Vantage Point." Can you tell why? Before reading further, study the two poems to see if you can find a tiny technical change in metrics, simple as the invention of the hammer, which helped the poet unlock his change in values, attitudes, and themes.

Back with me? Those two lines would not fit into "The Vantage Point" because each contains an anapest *(of the GIFT, at the HAND)*. Indeed, every line of "Mowing" contains at least one anapest and some have two. "The Vantage Point" contains not one. "The Vantage Point" is speckled with pyrrhics. "Mowing" has only one foot (*and did* in line 6) which can be read as either a pyrrhic or an iamb.

Let's go back over your scansions to make sure this matter is clear. "The Vantage Point" contains phrases such as *in the dawn* which look like anapests. But scansion of line 2 reveals that *in* must take a theoretical stress, making either a pyrrhic or iamb (as you prefer) of *me—in*. Every line of "The Vantage Point" has ten syllables, no more no less, which does not leave any room for anapests. Not one line of "Mowing" is decasyllabic. You can guess this at a glance by the way it sweeps wider on the page, though it is, like "The Vantage Point," in strict pentameter. "Mowing" spills over with unstressed syllables.

I mentioned in the last chapter two kinds of pyrrhics: those such as *me—in* which can take a theoretical stress on the second syllable, and those such as *To a* (line 3) which cannot. (One may imagine a theoretical stress on the *To,* making the foot a trochee; but one cannot read it as an iamb.) The pyrrhics of "The Vantage Point" tend to be the sort which can be read as iambs: *me—in, but to, et like, into,* and *er of.* Can you find all of these? Others must be read as trochees if they have any theoretical stress at all: *To a, on an,* and *but to.* This last one introduces an interesting sequence of two trochees:

i HAVE \ BUT to \ TURN on \ my ARM, \ and LO \

I indicate a stress on *but,* though I don't actually read it that way. One can hear in the line anapests overlaid on the iambic grain:

i HAVE \ but to TURN \ on my ARM, \ and LO \

Sounds a little like "Mowing," doesn't it? But we know Frost was too scrupulous with his metrics to have intended it as a four-foot line.

Read the poem aloud now, and notice how the first group of pyrrhics, the theoretical iambs, stands out. The meter forces you to give the second syllable of each a tiny stress, though you would not stress these syllables in conversational speech. Without the pyrrhics the meter would be monotonous, yet they force the lines into precious mannerism.

We are back to the question with which we began. What should we do with those little unstressed syllables that are so necessary to idiomatic speech, so deeply engrained in our language, but which water down our lines of poetry? To stress them simply brings attention to dullness. You can't get round them, yet if you use them in stress positions, they make the verse sound stilted and artificial. That may be all right if your purpose is to sound stilted and artificial, but in this case a young man was trying to outgrow such mannerism.

It seems as though he said to himself, at some point early in his career, "What the hell! I need a little slack!" So he used the syllables in anapests, making sure he had a strong stress (with one exception I will discuss later) for each foot, a stress that was natural to the language and important to the poem. We have seen that Chaucer, Shakespeare, Pope, and other poets who wrote in accentual syllabic meter used occasional anapests in iambic verse, but rarely and cautiously—sometimes using very artificial contractions such as *o'er* to avoid extra syllables.

John Donne, for instance, in the seventeenth century, strained against the limits of the decasyllabic line, using **elision** (leaving out syllables) and contractions to squeeze in unstressed syllables. One of his lines is "That I may rise, and stand, o'erthrow mee,'and bend." He seems to have wanted us to read the last part of the line as two iambs, as though pronounced *or THROW \ myan BEND \.* His contemporary, Ben Jonson, said he should be hanged for wrenching of meter, but, for me at least, the compression gives the line an agonizing emotional tension.

Frost apparently decided to incorporate anapests boldly, flagrantly, without apology. To make sure we sensed his deliberate intent, he put at least one in every line. He starts the first line with one. In one instance there are two in a row: *it it WHIS \ pered? i KNEW \.* Notice that the second of these is broken by a caesura. Otherwise there would be a danger that the anapests might run away with the line, making it jiggle and bounce and rush along like light verse.

Anapests speed the line whenever they occur (as in Pope's line about Camilla in the last chapter). They also make the texture of the poem somewhat relaxed and conversational. Frost was intent on capturing the sound of speech, keeping stresses where they belonged and off those annoying unstressed syllables. The stresses in "Mowing" are on plump and solid syllables, with the one exception I mentioned. Look at the second line:

> and THAT \ was my LONG \ SCYTHE WHIS \
>   per ing to \ the GROUND \

Either we read the three syllables as a **tribrach** (three unstressed syllables, ᴗᴗᴗ) or we force a bit of a stress onto *to*. I think the three stresses before the foot compensate for its slackness, and perhaps the rush of unstressed syllables captures the sound and feel of whispering.

Both poems are sonnets, and I will suggest that you look at them again when we study that form in Chapter 10. But you can notice some characteristics now. "The Vantage Point" looks boxy, tight, compressed, tidy with its little indentations, its precise and orthodox rhyme scheme. "Mowing" streams out, flaps like a banner, and its rhyme is unorthodox. The banner boldly stakes out a new aesthetic position. Frost wrote that way for the rest of his life, not with such persistent use of anapests, but with a commitment to natural speech and mature attitudes of engagement with life and reality.

Two lines are especially important in staking out his position: "Anything more than the truth would have seemed too weak." and: "The fact is the sweetest dream that labor knows." Isolated, they seem prosaic lines, devoid of imagery, rough in rhythm. Yet how powerful they are as a manifesto! The poem creates a context to make them work, intact, with their loose, whacking conversational force. They are nearly iambic. Frost might easily have revised them into lines that would fit into the meter of "The Vantage Point":

> Anything more than truth would seem too weak.

> Fact is the sweetest dream that labor knows.

Frost chose the other way. Why insist on those little extra syllables? The answer is in the poem. That's how people talk. That's fact. That's truth, which is stronger than truth decorated or trimmed to fit.

You will not write like Frost, but you will (if you are to become a good poet) probably settle upon a style, techniques, themes, which enable you to deal effectively with the central preoccupations of your life. For Frost it was a way to express his commitment to truth, to pleasure in labor, even to pain (look up his later poem, "To Earthward"). His manhood surges upon him in "Mowing," perhaps even more strongly than he would have recognized or acknowledged. The scythe in the swale is a sexual image, whether intended that way or not. As a Classical scholar he surely knew that the name of the flower, orchises, comes from the Greek word for testicles. (Compare the spikes of orchids with the delicate, single bluet in "The Vantage Point.") The orchises are uncannily juxtaposed with the quick flash of green snake. This is a strange, intense involvement with nature, quite in contrast to the view implied by looking from a superior position down the crater of the ant, or sniffing a plant that is bruisèd (with a marked accent to make us pronounce the word artifically). The speaker in "The Vantage Point" starts off tired, bored, looking for distraction and escape, wears out his attention in the first part of the poem and starts the second part bored again. It is the gesture of the limp wrist. In "Mowing" the poet finds what to do with his hands and body.

At the heart of the adaptation is what may seem a minute technical discovery, yet one which made all the difference: an occasional liberality with unstressed syllables. Neither Frost nor any other serious poet wants utter, unbridled freedom of form. He wants to "work easy in harness," to use one of Frost's phrases. Otherwise, why write poetry, instead of prose, at all? But the music he heard was that of common speech, and he needed some means of capturing it and heightening its effect, shaping its random cadences into art.

We are still talking about accentual syllabic verse in the early years of this century when poets were growing restless under its yoke. As a rule of thumb—whether you are talking about Shakespeare or Donne or Browning or Keats or Frost or almost any other poet using the form—about 60 percent of the feet of iambic verse are iambs. (Remember that for Pope the figure is nearer 80 percent.) But there is increasing roughness in much modern iambic verse, not so much because of the use of substitute feet, but because the pyrrhics are definitely pyrrhics (not theoretical iambs), the caesuras are more often off-center, there is increasing use of sharp enjambment. Here is some blank verse (unrhymed iambic pentameter) by Archibald MacLeish, the opening of his "Eleven":

And summer mornings the mute child, rebellious,
Stupid, hating the words, the meanings, hating
The Think now, Think, the O but Think! would leave
On tiptoe the three chairs on the verandah
And crossing tree by tree the empty lawn
Push back the shed door and upon the sill
Stand pressing out the sunlight from his eyes . . .

I will scan these lines so we may examine them together:

1   and SUM \ mer MOR \ nings the \ MUTE CHILD, \
    re BEL \ lious,
2   STUpid, \ HA ting \ the WORDS, \ the MEAN \
    ings, HA \ ting
3   the THINK \ now, THINK, \ the O \ but THINK! \
    would LEAVE \
4   on TIP \ toe the \ THREE CHAIRS \ on the \
    ver AN \ dah
5   and CROS \ sing TREE \ by TREE \ the EMP \
    ty LAWN \
6   PUSH BACK \ the SHED \ DOOR and \ uPON \
    the SILL \
7   STAND PRES \ sing OUT \ the SUN \ light from \
    his EYES \ . . .

This is basically the same meter as other iambic pentameter we have
looked at, with common variations. But MacLeish uses variations in
different places, and more frequently, than a poet such as Shakespeare
or Pope. There are thirty-five feet in the seven lines, of which I read
twenty-two as iambs, or about 63 percent. Notice that the third and fifth
lines are perfectly regular, and they stand out because they are so. The
third is a trick line, drawing sharp and annoying attention to that word
think which so torments the boy. Regularity drums it in. In the fifth line
regularity imitates the boy's passage across the lawn, tree-to-tree, light-
step-light.

Notice how the caesuras occur here and there, tossing with emotion.
Those toward the ends of lines are especially jolting, stopping us only to
push us round the corner with swift enjambment:

Stupid, // hating the words, // the meanings, // hating
The Think now, // Think, // the O but Think! // would leave
On tiptoe the three chairs on the verandah . . .

He doesn't want shapely, smooth, balanced lines such as were appropriate to Pope's rational discourse. Like an author of fiction, he creates tension, anxiety, the sullen mood and desperation of the child. Look at the pyrrhics. Three of them (one in the first line, two in the fourth) end with *the,* a word that normally cannot take a stress. The result is to put a greater strain on the even tenor of the line than the smooth pyrrhics with theoretical stresses of "The Vantage Point." The mid-line trochee in the sixth line almost jerks the meter out of kilter. Note that, like Pope, Frost reaffirms the regular beat at the end of the line, only to vary it at the beginning of the next.

Yet this is fairly conventional iambic pentameter. When MacLeish loosens the meter even further, the underlying iambic beat may at times almost disappear. Here is the opening of his "Epistle to Be Left in the Earth":

. . . It is colder now
                      there are many stars
                                we are drifting
North by the Great Bear
                  the leaves are falling
The water is stone in the scooped rocks
                               to southward
Red sun gray air
              the crows are
Slow on their crooked wings
                  the jays have left us

All new lines begin at the left margin, the drops indicating continuations of the same lines. Try scanning the lines yourself before checking against my scansion:

```
        . . . it is COLD \ er NOW \
                    there are MAN \ y STARS \
                              we are DRIFT \ ing
        NORTH by \ the GREAT \ BEAR the \
                              LEAVES are FALL \ ing
        the WA \ ter is STONE \ in the \ SCOOPED ROCKS \
                              to SOUTH \ ward
        x RED \ x SUN \ x GRAY \ x AIR \
                              the CROWS \ are
        SLOW on \ their CROOK \ ed WINGS \
                              the JAYS \ have LEFT \ us
```

What are those little *x*'s? I use them to indicate missing syllables. These
are monosyllabic feet—necessarily read that way to fill out the five-beat
pattern established so clearly by the rest of the poem. And notice I said
beat, not *stress,* for when verse becomes as irregular as this, it is moving
toward accentual rather than accentual syllabic meter. In the early twen-
tieth century most major poets, including not only Frost and MacLeish,
but Pound, Cummings, Eliot, Stevens, and many others, loosened the
meter by using more variations such as we have seen. This resulted in a
kind of mixture of accentual and accentual syllabic meters in which
beats were more significant than metrical feet. But these poets con-
tinually drew on the harmonies of accentual syllabic, alternating stress
as well.

Consider, for instance, those **monosyllabic** feet (sometimes called
truncated feet, or, when they occur in falling rhythms, that is, in trochaic
or dactylic verse, **catalectic** feet). At the end of Chapter 5 we noticed
that such feet sometimes occur in folk poetry, songs, and light verse,
especially at the beginnings of lines (or, in falling rhythms, at the ends of
lines). These (in rising rhythms) are called **headless** lines, such as:

```
        x MAR \ y HAD \ a LIT \ tle LAMB \
```

Monosyllabic feet used internally in a line distort the meter. One's
natural instinct is to combine them with other syllables to form more
normal feet, throwing off the count of feet. For example, MacLeish's
line, "Red sun gray air the crows are," looks as though it starts with two

spondees, and we can tell that these are monosyllabic feet only by the metrical context. All the other lines have five feet, so it is highly unlikely that MacLeish meant this one to be read as shorter. The four monosyllabic feet in a row slow down the line, creating a sense of space between the stresses, suggesting the awesome hush of contemplation of mysterious changes in the climate. Modern poets have increasingly used monosyllabic feet to give effects of primitive naivete, deliberate roughness, or dramatic hesitation.

The first two lines use a striking number of anapests. Verse which is predominately anapestic (such as the limerick) tends to be comic or light. It is often used in children's poetry. But in this poem and much of his other work MacLeish uses frequent anapests and yet maintains a serious tone. The device becomes almost a trademark of his verse. (Compare Whitman's use of dactylic, or falling, rhythm.) This is hard to do without letting the line skip away into lightness. A helpful guideline is that you should avoid using two or more anapests or trochees in succession (in generally iambic verse) except when you want them for a definite, special effect. Both anapests and trochees are so powerful they tend to set up their own tune, and you lose control of the beat if you use them indiscriminately. Notice that in his first line MacLeish separates the two anapests with an iamb. In "Eleven" he uses two trochees together ("Stupid, hating . . .") and the whole line seems disturbingly trochaic.

"Epistle" is a poem from the 1920s. MacLeish's audience had been overexposed to the accentual syllabic poetry of the nineteenth century. To bring freshness and vitality to tired forms, poets began taking more and more liberties with the basic pattern of alternating stress. They could depend upon their audience's hearing scraps of old rhythms, like strains from half-remembered tunes. Readers would not, of course, scan the poems as we have been doing, but if one is attuned to meter, one knows when it is there, even though strained or subdued. Today, however, readers are likely to miss subtleties of meter altogether.

In Chapter 4, Auden's four-beat accentual poem, "Petition," was considered. We saw the poet straining to get intellectual, polysyllabic language into the thumping form of Old English meter, with uncertain success. Such a line is easier to control if it is shorter—two beats or three rather than four. Auden's "September 1, 1939" is much more effective metrically (and otherwise) than "Petition." It is still basically accentual, but, as we will see, it draws on some of the harmonies of accentual syllabic meter as well:

> I sit in one of the dives
> On Fifty-second Street
> Uncertain and afraid
> As the clever hopes expire
> Of a low dishonest decade:
> Waves of anger and fear
> Circulate over the bright
> And darkened lands of the earth,
> Obsessing our private lives:
> The unmentionable odour of death
> Offends the September night.

This is the first of nine stanzas of eleven lines each. There is no definite rhyme pattern, but most lines rhyme (often with off-rhymes, discussed in Chapter 7), and each stanza concludes with a rhyme (here *bright/night*). The poem's form is, like its content, casual but tense, free yet sharply disciplined.

Why do I call it a blend of accentual and accentual syllabic meters? There is only one line which cannot be scanned as trimeter in a combination of various accentual syllabic feet:

> the un MEN \ tion a ble O \ dour of DEATH \

And the extra syllable in the second foot may well be slurred past in a conversational reading. But iambs, trochees, and anapests are interspersed so irregularly that the pump of beats generally drowns out the regularity of alternating stress:

> i SIT \ in ONE \ of the DIVES \
> on FIF \ ty SEC \ ond STREET \
> un CER \ tain and \ a FRAID \
> as the CLE \ ver HOPES \ ex PIRE \
> of a LOW \ dis HON \ est dec ADE. \
> x WAVES \ of AN \ ger and FEAR \
> CIRC u \ late O \ ver the BRIGHT \

and DARK \ ened LANDS \ of the EARTH, \
ob SES \ sing our PRI \ vate LIVES: \
the un MEN \ tion a ble O \ dour of DEATH \
of FENDS \ the sep TEM \ ber NIGHT \

The preferred pronunciation of *decade* is with the stress on the first syllable, but the rhyme here draws it to the second, an acceptable pronunciation. If these lines were strictly accentual, such a line as the third would have to be read as a two-beat rather than three-beat line. If it were strictly accentual syllabic, the tenth line would be awkward. I am sure Auden simply thought of it as a roughly three-beat line, but often, throughout the poem, one of the beats disappears into what would have to be scanned as a pyrrhic in accentual syllabic meter. Of course he might also have thought of it as a poem of three-beat lines with occasional two-beat lines as variations, but in that case it is odd that these lines always supply pyrrhics which can take up the beat with a theoretical stress, for example, *a BOUT \ de MOC \ ra cy.* \ The variations are never so extreme as to throw off seriously a reading in alternating stress. For example, when monosyllabic feet occur (as in line 6 above, or, later, in *x WHO \ can REACH \ the DEAF* \), they are always in the first foot, making the lines headless, whereas they would be much more disruptive elsewhere in the line (and much more characteristic of purely accentual meter).

This is obviously a scrupulously crafted poem, and Auden was so meticulous a technician that it would be a mistake to interpret any detail of it as accidental when any other explanation can be found. I hope you will look it up and study its content as well as its form, since its fearful prophecy at the outbreak of World War II still disturbs us with both its realistic nightmare and idealistic dream:

There is no such thing as the State
And no one exists alone;
Hunger allows no choice
To the citizen or the police;
We must love one another or die.

That is a position from which Auden retreated as he grew more conservative politically and religiously, and he dropped the stanza containing these lines from collections of his poems. But the lines, once uttered, have a strength greater than the will of their creator. Our culture will remember Auden more enduringly for this poem, and especially for these lines he rejected, than for anything else he wrote.

From this poem you can derive guidelines which will help you understand the form of much modern poetry and help you shape your own work. Once grounded in accentual syllabic meter, you can vary it freely, especially in the direction of increasing the number of anapests, spondees, trochees, and monosyllabic feet over the norms of historical practice. It may help you to think in terms of beats rather than feet, remembering that you can lighten their tendency toward heavy thumping with pyrrhics that can take theoretical stress. You can loosen the line, as we have seen Frost, MacLeish, and Auden do, on the basis of sophisticated understanding of the alternatives possible in various meters (and of the dangers implicit in each), but you cannot well do this on the basis of ignorance. Your lines will go limp and dissolve into prose.

You should be aware of another problem as well. I mentioned that the readers of poets in the early part of the century had been saturated with the accentual syllabic poetry of the nineteenth century, so they could hear those old harmonies when the poets took liberties in mixing them. But today our readers have been saturated with free verse and have little ear for meter at all. For them the painstaking pentameter of MacLeish or trimeter of Auden may fall on deaf ears. Recently I saw a striking poster including the text of W. B. Yeats's great poem (in iambic pentameter), "The Second Coming." Under it was impertinently printed, "FREE VERSE." It is a sign of the times. How the ghost of Yeats must have groaned. As that poem says, "Mere anarchy is loosed upon the earth."

Our problem as poets is to reawaken a sensitivity to the forms of poetry, and this may require a more conservative practice than that of the great poets who broke new metrical ground in our century. For readers to catch subtleties, they first have to hear the obvious. We have to find a compromise between stiff artificiality and careless conversational ease. Pope's was a poetry of the era of the minuet—of extremely mannered and symmetrical style. He regarded his polished couplets as "following Nature." But what seems natural to one era seems highly unnatural to another. Freedom itself is a meaningless and empty concept. We may think we have freedom on a modern dance floor, but the popularity of discotheque styles is channeling that freedom in directions of new restraint. We do not currently have the freedom to dance a minuet. Styles are always regarded as "natural," no matter how strange they may be, and they are always confining.

Modernist poets, for all their freedom, no longer speak to a wide audience; they seem to have drifted away from the music of language and not to have developed modes that can sustain narrative and dramatic poetry or deal comprehensibly and effectively with major themes. It is a challenge I hope you will respond to with creative force.

7

Ringing the Changes

Alliteration and Sound Echoes

All distinctions between poetry and prose involve matters of degree. The most absolute is that poetry generally uses the line as a unit, but prose does not. However, there are exceptions. **Prose poems** are intense, lyrical paragraphs which do not use line units. On the other hand, advertising, headlines, charts, and other prose forms do use the line as a unit.

All we can say is that poetry *tends* to differ from prose in certain ways. For example, in earlier chapters we noted that poetry in English tends to use more words of Germanic derivation, to use stresses more frequently and with greater regularity, to use concrete, as opposed to abstract, language, and to use line units that tend toward accentual syllabic meter, specifically toward, five-foot lines of alternating, rising stress. This chapter will deal with manipulation of sound values other than stress. Poetry tends toward repetition of sounds, often in patterns.

Rhyme is a general term for all varieties of sound repetition, though *true rhyme* (discussed in the next chapter) is a very specific case with an exact definition. **Alliteration** is, thus, really a kind of rhyme. The term refers to the repetition of individual sounds for artistic effect, whereas rhyme usually implies groups of sounds. You will sometimes hear terms referring to different kinds of alliteration. **Consonance** is the repetition of consonant sounds; **assonance** is the repetition of vowel sounds.

When a recognizable group of sounds (as opposed to individual sounds) echo one another but do not make a true rhyme, the repetition is called an **off-rhyme.** There are many kinds of off-rhymes; almost any repetition of sounds may be called by this name. But two specific kinds of off-rhyme are defined by repeated consonants or repeated vowels. When the consonant sounds echo, but the vowels are different in sound, the off-rhyme is called a **consonantal rhyme.** Some consonantal rhymes have identical sounds, some have only partially corresponding sounds, some have consonantal sounds in reversed order, and so on: *beat/bat, crisp/clasp, spin/naps, crow/crane.* **Assonantal rhymes** may have identical or nearly similar vowel sounds, but their consonants are different: *bladder/fatten, bait/rain, could/howl.*

We most often think of rhymes occurring at the ends of lines **(end-rhyme).** Off-rhymes such as I have illustrated often take the place of true rhymes in end-rhyme positions. As will be discussed in the next chapter, the pattern of end-rhymes, whether they be off-rhymes or true rhymes, tends to be related to the overall structure of the poem. Rhymes which occur within lines are called **internal rhymes.** These may be patterned, occurring regularly in mid-line positions:

> All night he flew till day was new
> And the sun was rising fair;
> Still ocean rolled its depths untold
> Beneath him everywhere.

These are special effects. But unpatterned internal rhyme and alliteration weave the fabric, or provide the texture of poetry. In this chapter we will look at some of the ways these unpatterned echoes of sound work to create rich harmony in good poetry.

I have often said, especially in discussing meter, that, as a poet, you have to learn to hear language apart from its meaning. Of course the sounds should be appropriate to the meaning (in Pope's phrase, "an echo to the sense"). But there is more to it than mere imitation of sounds or echoing. At the simplest level we have **onomatopoeia,** the deliberate imitation of sounds by words: *buzz, bang, crunch,* and so forth. Suppose that your poem is describing sawing a board. You might want onomatopoetic words to catch the screech of the downstroke, the burr of the saw's return. You might also want the rhythm to reflect the heavy steady labor. But what sounds carry the whiff of resin, the salty joy of sweat, the breath of sun on your back? How will the language change in the cool of evening when you are sipping cider by firelight, in a mood of reflection, the conversation nodding into silence as a log whispers and colors subside with the light? You need all the resources of language— the connotations of words, the variety of phrasal structures, the interplay of sounds—to imitate and create the total experience.

Some people are better than others at arranging a room for taste and comfort, some at knowing and combining the ingredients of a good dinner, not only the food but the table and the company. And some seem to have a knack for making phrases that are memorable, that ring, that hang together, that stir the imagination and evoke complex responses from listeners and readers. When we take language apart, as we will do here, we look at everything that goes into such phrase-making. If you already have the knack, you may not need to look so closely at the details of how the sounds of language work together. But, nonetheless, I think it will help in sharpening your sensibility and developing that knack into a skill you can use with certainty.

If you read (as I do) a great deal of relatively unskilled poetry, you may find it difficult to say just why it is not effective. There are always many reasons, but when you find a poem in the batch which stands out, which, by contrast with what you have been reading, suddenly sounds like poetry, you are probably responding to sound texture. How can I illustrate this? I open an anthology of modern poetry at random and happen on a poem of thirteen lines of blank verse. I like it. Now I rewrite that poem in the same number of lines and approximately the same meter. But I try to write as though I had no ear for language. I shuffle the two versions. Here they are. Can you tell which was written by Theodore Roethke and which is my pale imitation?

Dolor

I have known the inexorable sadness of pencils,
Neat in their boxes, dolor of pad and paper-weight,
All the misery of manila folders and mucilage,
Desolation in immaculate public places,
Lonely reception room, lavatory, switchboard,
The unalterable pathos of basin and pitcher,
Ritual of multigraph, paper-clip, comma,

Endless duplication of lives and objects.
And I have seen dust from the walls of institutions,
Finer than flour, alive, more dangerous than silica,
Sift, almost invisible, through long afternoons of tedium,
Dropping a fine film on nails and delicate eyebrows,
Glazing the pale hair, the duplicate grey standard faces.

Dolor

I am aware of inescapable grief
Of pencils neat in boxes, paper-weights,
The dolor of pads, folders, clips and glue,
The loneliness in crowds and public buildings,
The sadness at the drinking fountain, all
The rituals of copying machines
That duplicate our lives as they do commas.
There is a dust in all these sterile offices
Which is, although invisible, alive,
More dangerous than silica. It sifts
Like flour over tedious afternoons
And leaves a filmy coat on nails and eyebrows,
Turning the fine hair glassy, the faces grey.

As a review of the last chapter, you might try scanning the two versions. You should be able to find five feet in each line of both. Why does the first look longer on the page? What material does it include that is not in the second? Which poem is easier to comprehend? Is that necessarily better—or worse? Which, overall, seems to you the better poem?

I think that if Roethke's poem didn't exist, my version (the second) would be considered a passable poem—one that might well appear in a literary magazine. And if you preferred it to the first, I think I can understand why. Some might object to Roethke's fancy vocabulary, his abundant adjectives, and his loose meter. But do you also hear the flatness of the second version? If you want to be not merely a competent poet but an excellent one, you have to look past the idea (which is approximately the same in both versions) to the intensity and force of the language, especially to the music of Roethke's phrases.

His first line starts with an anapestic sweep that makes it seem to have only four feet, but there is a pyrrhic tucked in *inexorable*. It is a dramatic, heroic opening, coming to an almost humorous conclusion with the word *pencils*. Surprise. One is engaged. But let's look at the sound texture in detail. Notice, first, the *n* sounds—five in the first line, one at the beginning of the next. Now the **sibilants**—a term used for sounds that hiss in the teeth, *sh, s, z*. The *x* in *inexorable* is a combination of a *k* sound and an *s*. We hear it again in *boxes*. Thus there are seven *s* sounds in the first line and a half. The term **plosives** is used for sounds that require a complete stop, a closure of the oral passage, *p, b*. The first comes with *pencils*, and that idea is rounded off with *boxes*, reinforced by the alliteration of *pads* and *paper-weights*. Plosives are closely related to **dentals**—consonants made with the tongue against the teeth, *t, d, th*. Four dentals occur in the second line.

Do poets pay attention to all that? Of course not—not in any conscious way. They may not even know these phonetic terms such as sibilants, plosives, dentals, and others I will define here. But if you look closely at good poetry you will notice a tendency for sounds to cluster or to relate to one another in ways that do not occur in ordinary speech or writing. The terms, like those of metrics, simply help us talk about a phenomenon that occurs in poetry. Look at my version of "Dolor," in which I was deliberately paying no attention to the interplay of sounds. Surely you can find some groupings of sounds—partly because I used many of the same words Roethke used. But they do not echo one another so richly; they are not as likely to hold phrases, lines, ideas, or passages together in the way they do in Roethke's poem.

One of the most obvious passages of alliteration is in Roethke's third and fourth lines—this string of *m*'s. Consonants sounded through the nose (*m, n, ng*) are called **nasals,** and these *m*'s pick up on the effect of the *n*'s we noticed in the first and second lines. Alliteration is especially noticeable to the eye at the beginnings of words and to the ear at the beginnings of stressed syllables. In line 3, the *m*'s in *misery* and *mucilage*, and, in line 4, in *immaculate*, strike the ear with more force than does the *m* in *manila*, which begins an unstressed syllable. Poets tend to avoid excessive alliteration of stressed syllables or beginnings of words unless they are being funny. There is, indeed, a touch of humor, of the mock-heroic, in talking about the inexorable sadness of pencils and the misery of manila folders and mucilage. The nasals occurring in unstressed positions in these first four lines have a different effect from the string of obvious *m*'s. They make the lines sing.

A new sound begins to emerge in these lines—that of **liquids,** those vowel-like consonants that are pronounced without friction, *l, r.* They are frequent but subdued in lines 3 and 4, then well up in the next four lines:

> Lonely reception room, lavatory, switchboard,
> The unalterable pathos of basin and pitcher,
> Ritual of multigraph, paper-clip, comma,
> Endless duplication of lives and objects.

One might call the sound of this passage lugubrious. Did you notice, by the way, that the whole poem tends toward a falling rhythm? All the lines have **feminine endings** (that is, they end with hypermetrical, unstressed syllables), and most begin with trochees. The falling tendency has its own lugubrious effect! The plosives, *p* and *b* sounds, are also prominent in these lines, continuing the pattern we saw in the opening. After the hard sounds of *objects,* however, they almost disappear.

There is a change in the tone of the poem beginning with the ninth line—and the sounds change accordingly. The lines are longer, with more syllables, though they still have five feet. The poem is structured almost like a sonnet, with an octave, or eight-line opening, and a five-line (instead of six-line, as is usual in sonnets) resolution. The first eight lines observe the sadness of institutional and office life. The last five examine the human consequences in dangerous, dull conformity. The eighth line, with its key word *duplication,* prepares us for this new tone and new idea.

What kinds of alliteration do you notice in the last five lines? You may be especially struck by the **fricatives,** consonants that derive their sound from friction between the breath and teeth or lips—especially *f* and *v* sounds, but the sibilants (*s, z, sh*) also are sounds caused by friction. The tone is softer than it was in the first eight lines. Our attention is now upon the dust, finer than flour, alive, which sifts, almost invisible, leaving its fine film. Roethke said "Dropping a fine film." I think *leaving* might have been a more effective word in creating this effect—but, then, Roethke was probably not aware he was creating it.

I have been drawing your attention to consonants, but let's now consider the vowels in this passage. Linguists classify the fourteen vowel sounds of our language according to where the jaw is, where the tongue is, and whether or not the lips are rounded when they are pronounced. Say *bit, bet, bat.* Do you feel your jaw dropping to a successively lower position for each word? The vowels in these words are called, respectively, **high, mid,** and **low vowels.** Now pay attention to your tongue as you say *bet, but, boat.* Do you feel it pulling back for each vowel? These vowels are called, respectively, **front, central,** and **back vowels.** Each vowel is classified according to both sets of terms: The vowel in *bought* is a low, back vowel; that in *bat* is a low, front vowel. For both vowels the jaw is low, but the tongue is forward for one, back for the other. Some vowels spelled usually with one letter are, in fact, diphthongs. They are made up of two sounds which blur together. For example, the vowel in *bite* (or *I,* or *finer,* or *alive*) is actually two vowels, *ah-ee,* a low, central vowel followed by a high, front vowel. Actually many, or even most of our vowels are pronounced as diphthongs in ordinary speech. You can feel your jaw or tongue (or both) moving as you pronounce them. Listen (and feel) the *a* sounds in *dangerous, nails, glazing, pale, grey, faces.* I pronounce them as two sounds, *eh-ee,* blending into one.

These fine distinctions may not concern you as a poet, but you should be tuned in to repetitions of the same or similar vowel sounds. Listen to the insistence of the *ih* sound in words close together such as *silica, sift, invisible, institutions, delicate, duplicate.* The repetitions keep your jaw returning to that high, front position. And notice the difference when the jaw drops and the tongue retreats. Do you hear that dust drift down to the depths of *through long afternoons, Dropping, eyebrows?* The pattern is not consistent, and the poet may not have been consciously aware of it at all. *Finer* and *flour* have, respectively, stressed high and low vowel sounds. (That of *flour,* like the *o* in *eyebrows,* is another made up of two sounds: *ah-oo.*) *Tedium* has two high vowels and a low one. Roethke was not trying to prove a point, or be a virtuoso of vowels. But he listened to his language, savored his phrases, thought about that dust sifting, and, probably, by intuition alone, chose words that whispered with soft fricatives and vowels that gently settled.

I have by no means discussed every instance of sound repetition in the poem. Take it phrase by phrase and listen: "Sift, almost invisible"—how the *s*'s and, especially, the stressed *ih* sounds interplay. "Long afternoons

of tedium"—how the nasals sing, the vowels—*aw, a, oo, uh, ee, ee, uh*—
ripple around the low notes. See how often a stressed sound early in the
line alliterates with one late in the line—*Dropping-delicate, Glazing-grey.*
(Incidentally, *g* and *k* sounds are called **gutturals,** pronounced low in
the throat.) All this may seem very technical, and you will certainly not
write much poetry thinking about nasals and dentals and low vowels.
But when you find a passage of poetry that seems to you especially effec-
tive you might want to analyze it in this way to discover how the lines
work. And if your own material seems flat to your ear (or to an impartial
reader), you probably need to spend a good bit of time listening to these
subtle tunes.

You can overdo it, of course. Too fastidious a concern with sound,
like too fastidious a scansion of meter, can distract you from other im-
portant elements of poetry. And if you play too many games with sounds
you will distract your reader.

Furthermore, tastes change with time. Old English poetry, as we have
seen, incorporated an alliterative pattern in its metrical structure. Welsh
poetry uses alliteration in very specific patterns. Gerard Manley
Hopkins was strongly influenced by both Old English and Welsh
poetry, and his poetry is exuberantly alliterative, excessively so for
many readers. A precious literary style of Shakespeare's time, **euphu-
ism,** used heavy alliteration, which Shakespeare satirized both in the
title and in much of the poetry of *Love's Labour's Lost.* Algernon Charles
Swinburne was much teased for his addiction to alliteration, and he
satirized himself in "Nephelidia," which begins:

> From the depth of the dreamy decline of the dawn through a
>   notable nimbus of nebulous noonshine,
>   Pallid and pink as the palm of the flag-flower that flickers
>   with fear of the flies as they float,
> Are the looks of our lovers that lustrously lean from a
>   marvel of mystic miraculous moonshine,
>   These that we feel in the flood of our blushes that thicken
>   and threaten with throbs through the throat?

The monotonous anapestic octameter does much to enhance the tedium
of verbal cleverness. Most readers today prefer subtler effects. Use
alliteration of initial sounds of stressed syllables sparingly. Work instead

with sound clusters, variations, interplay. Mere mechanical repetition is a bore.

Similar considerations apply to the use of internal rhyme. When such rhyme is patterned, as I mentioned at the beginning of this chapter, it has much the same effect as end-rhyme (discussed in the next chapter). Here is the second stanza of Edgar Allan Poe's "The Raven":

> Ah, distinctly I remember it was in the bleak December;
> And each separate dying ember wrought its ghost upon the
>   floor.
> Eagerly I wished the morrow;—vainly I had sought to
>   borrow
> From my books surcease of sorrow—sorrow for the lost
>   Lenore—
> For the rare and radiant maiden whom the angels named
>   Lenore—
>   Nameless *here* for evermore.

Each octameter line is in two parts, broken after the fourth foot. In the first line the word before the caesura rhymes with the word at the end of the line. The same rhyme is picked up in the word before the caesura in the second, and so on. This intricate scheme is not followed in every stanza, but the interplay of rhymes at the caesuras and ends of lines is complex, ingenious, and rather tedious, as it attracts attention to the rhyming at the expense of sense. Such devices work better in comic verse.

But internal rhyming is more subdued (and I think less annoying) when unpatterned, and when true rhymes are varied with off-rhymes. Internal rhymes are thick in one of my early poems, "Hobbes and the Ghosts." In this passage the old philosopher is thinking about his young female secretary:

> My mind has never fumbled
> like my ancient hands: platonic hands, too old
> for loving, blurring the gesture, frightening her
> who loves me in the sunlight when I talk.
> We walk our walk. She stands all dumb with life
> while I am turning, deep in water toiling,

> head alive with trim moustaches, points
> of fire beneath my bushy head of ashes,
> then puts away my hand as though it were
> a wisp of hair that brushed her cheek, distraction
> in a maiden's summer morning. Our last years
> we hold the young ones by the ears. We want
> too much—that they should listen to our talk
> and bear our palsied touch.

By burying one of each rhyme pair internally and putting the other at the end of a line, I hoped to retain the effect of end-rhyme while offsetting the tendency of end-rhymed poetry to jingle. (Do you find the pairs? *talk/walk, moustaches/ashes, years/ears, much/touch?*) Other rhymes (for example, *hands/stands, hair/bear*) are completely buried. Repetition of words (*hand, hands, walk* three times; *talk* twice; *life, alive, head* twice; and so on) reinforces the effect of subdued echoing. Off-rhymes (*blurring/her, fire/hair/were,* and so on) further deepen the alliterative texture.

That was written over thirty years ago, so I cannot report exactly what was going through my mind, but I do know that these sound patterns were quite deliberate. I have spoken here of the "intuition" poets have for threading their work with interesting and effective sound patterns, but that intuition is sharpened by conscious attention and learning. Especially in the early stages of my career I put much creative energy into listening to how sounds fell together, how the tone of a passage shifted as one emphasized one consonant group (such as fricatives or gutturals) or vowel group (such as high, front vowels) and then another, how rhymes and off-rhymes could be slipped in without attracting too much attention to themselves or could be emphasized for special effects.

When you appreciate such effects, in your reading as well as in your writing, you are truly beginning to grasp poetry. You are learning to value language for itself, not merely for what it says, not merely for its message.

This does not mean that you value it for sound effects alone. That, too, has been tried. (You may be sure that poets, like other artists, will try everything possible in their medium.) Dadaist poets in the early years of this century published journals and books of poetry consisting of lines that sounded like "Gobble gabble grobble glib / glaggle burble babble bib." Somewhat more interesting were the sound effects of Edith Sitwell's *Façade*. Here is a short excerpt:

> Said King Pompey the emperor's age,
> Shuddering black in his temporal cape
> Of dust, "The dust is everything—
> The heart to love and the voice to sing,
> Indianapolis,
> And the Acropolis . . .

The poet explained this passage:

> In the first two lines, the sound rises. "Pompey," in sound, is a dark distorted shadow of "Emperor" and of its crouching echo, "temporal"—a shadow upside down, one might say, for in "Emperor" the sound dies down in hollow darkness, whereas in "Pompey" it begins in thick muffling animal darkness and then rises, dying away into a little thin whining air. The crazy reversed sound of "Indianapolis," "Acropolis"—"Acropolis" being a hollow darkened echo of "Indianapolis," broken down and toppling over into the abyss—this effect is deliberate.

I hope my discussion of sound manipulation has not sounded as nonsensical and subjective to you as Edith Sitwell's does to me. Surely it is meaning, after all, which makes poetry endure, and when meaning is abandoned altogether, language becomes merely absurd. There is a kind of nursery-rhyme delight in the bippety-boppety-boo effects of pure sound, but it soon wears thin. Rather, you want to be able to create a rich and enduring fabric of sound to receive and give depth and body to your tapestry of sense.

8

The Sculp of Rhyme

End Rhymes

When most people speak of rhyme they are not talking about the kinds of alliteration, sound echoes, and internal rhyme discussed in the last chapter, but about **end-rhyme,** the use of rhymes at the ends of lines, often in a pattern related to the structure of the poem. Some regard anything that rhymes as a poem and anything that doesn't as not a poem. On the other hand there are literary magazines which automatically reject any rhymed poem as a jingle, no matter how high its quality. But the traditions of rhymed and unrhymed poetry in our language are equally ancient and strong. The fashion now seems to be swinging back toward rhyme. In any case, it is important that poets understand rhyme thoroughly. Nothing stands out more awkwardly in amateur work than bad rhyming.

In good poetry, off-rhymes (discussed in the last chapter) are as commonly used as true rhymes. What hurts the ear are the near-misses. Start with the understanding of exactly what a **true rhyme** is: *one in which the first sounds of the last stressed syllables of the rhyming words are different and all subsequent sounds are the same.* Each detail of that definition is important and needs discussion.

What is the last stressed syllable? The word *photographer* has four syllables. In ordinary speech the second syllable, *tog,* is the only one stressed. We could say *geographer* rhymed with it because *og* (the second, and only stressed, syllable in the word) begins with a different sound from *tog,* and all subsequent sounds are the same. That would be a **trisyllabic rhyme** because three syllables are involved in the rhyming: *ographer* and *tographer.* But trisyllabic rhymes are used only in comic poetry such as limericks or the patter songs of Gilbert and Sullivan. They attract too much attention to self-conscious ingenuity to be effective in serious poetry.

Does this mean that such words as *photographer* and *geographer* cannot be used in rhyming positions in serious poetry? By no means! If you listen closely you will hear a distinction in stress in the last two syllables, a distinction your dictionary does not indicate. The *pher* in each is somewhat more stressed than the *ra* which precedes it. Therefore *ra pher* can be read as an iamb or pyrrhic with a theoretical stress. In that case you are considering *pher* as the last stressed syllable, and since this syllable starts with the same sound in both *photographer* and *geographer,* the words do *not* rhyme. They are **identicals.** They work as trisyllabic rhymes but not as **monosyllabic rhymes,** that is, rhymes in which only one syllable is involved in the rhyming.

Confusing? Well, this may not be much of a limerick, but it works so far as the rhymes are concerned:

> There once was a lusty photographer
> Who was snapping a pretty stenographer.
> She said, "What you're doing
> Is more than just viewing.
> You're mapping me like a geographer!"

Tog, nog, and *og* all start with different sounds (as do *do* and *view*), and the subsequent sounds in each case are the same as those of the words they rhyme with. The first, second, and fifth lines are (as in all limericks) trimeter. The unstressed syllables at the end of each, *ra-pher,* are hypermetrical. Just for kicks I threw in an internal rhyme, *snapping* and *mapping,* which is not part of the pattern. In comic poetry you might as well have all the fun you can.

To use such a word for a monosyllabic rhyme in trimeter, you make the hypermetrical syllables part of the meter:

> when a LUS \ ty pho TOG \ ra PHER \

Let's try that in a limerick:

> When a lusty photographer
> Starts to snap a stenographer
> With some hocus-pocus
> He may shift his focus
> To snapping that he may prefer.

Now lines 1, 2, and 5 end in identicals, generally considered defects in serious poetry, though in comic verse anything goes (that works).

Don't be confused by spelling: *fer* and *pher* are the same sound. *Speak* rhymes with *antique,* but *teak* does not. Here are some pairs of words. Which ones rhyme, and why do the others not rhyme?

1	assault/basalt	6	grown/groan
2	terrible/unbearable	7	then/burden
3	photographing/telegraphing	8	believe/relieve
4	retrograde/ambuscades	9	expose/San Jose
5	mansion/overrun	10	degenerate/incriminate

1. Both stressed syllables begin with *s*—an identical.

2. Acceptable as a trisyllabic rhyme, for *ter* and *bear* begin with different sounds; unacceptable as a monosyllabic rhyme, since the *ble*'s are identical. But either of these words could be a monosyllabic rhyme with *full, wool,* or *masterful.*

3. Nope. Both words have a primary stress on their first syllables, *pho* and *tel,* which do not rhyme, and a secondary stress on their third syllables, both *graph,* which are identicals.

4. Both *grade* and *scades* take secondary stresses, so this would be a rhyme if it weren't for the final *s.* This kind of near-miss is jangling. It is better to use a definite off-rhyme, such as *retrograde* with such words as *crude, deride,* or *flake,* than to use two words which differ only in that one has a final *s* or *ed.* Such rhymes look as though the poet just couldn't quite make it work and settled for a careless approximation, whereas off-rhymes are at least unobtrusive and seem deliberate.

5. The stress is on the first syllable of one, the last of the other. Ouch!

6. An identical.

7. Do you say *bur-DEN?*

8. An identical.

9. If the first word were a noun it should be printed with an accent mark, *exposé,* and would rhyme with San Jose. But without the accent mark it rhymes with *SAN JOE'S.* This pair might be considered an **eye rhyme,** one which looks like a rhyme because of its spelling, but does not rhyme when pronounced. In earlier centuries poets sometimes used eye rhymes such as *love/prove,* but poets today rarely use them.

10. I am throwing you a double curve here. What part of speech is *degenerate?* If you use it as a noun or adjective ("she is a degenerate"; "she is a degenerate woman"), the primary stress is on the second syllable. If you look it up in the dictionary, you will see that neither of the last two syllables is given even a secondary stress, and the vowel in the last syllable is a schwa, a neutral *uh* sound, which does not rhyme with *fate* or *locate.*

Such rhymes (I call them **weak rhymes** and will discuss them more thoroughly later in this chapter) are, however, often used by good poets. Compare this word with the discussion of the rhymes of *photographer* and with the *ble* rhymes in (2) above. Even when used as a noun or adjective, *degenerate* has slightly more stress on the last syllable than on the one before it, so might be considered a theoretical iamb. If it is used this way, the *a* sound is drawn out and lifted, so it does make a passable rhyme with *fate* or *locate.* This is a convention of accentual syllabic poetry, and it is essential that you understand it in order to hear properly poetry of the past, or to write well accentual syllabic poetry of your own.

But that is only one twist of the curve. In spite of what I have said above, *degenerate* as a noun or adjective sounds awkward when rhymed with a word so similar in sound as *incriminate:*

> What man is so degenerate
> He would his wife incriminate?

The problem is that *incriminate* is a verb and *degenerate* also *can* be a verb. Used as a verb, it is an acceptable rhyme:

> When civil men degenerate,
> Their actions will incriminate
> The honored leaders of the state.

All three rhyme words have a stress on the final syllable.

Whether used as a noun, adjective, or verb, the primary stress is on *gen*. Therefore, *degenerate* can also be used as a trisyllabic rhyme (but not with *incriminate,* since *crim* does not rhyme with *gen*):

> Don't ask me, now, to venerate
> A man who's so degenerate
> He slobbers on his dinner plate
> And nods asleep at ten or eight . . .

Did you catch the bad rhyme there? In the third line, *din* does not rhyme with *ven, gen,* and *ten,* and *er plate* does not have the same sound as *erate* and *or eight.* How about making the last line end "ten of eight"? Better sense, worse rhyme. But one of the masters of trisyllabic rhymes was W. S. Gilbert (of Gilbert and Sullivan), who rhymed "animal or mineral" with his "modern major general," so I guess imperfection does not matter too much in this kind of verse.

Ingenious rhymes attract attention to themselves and away from serious content, but they are lots of fun. How many words can you think of that end with *irmy?* I could find only three, and that challenge alone prompted a limerick:

> The bear in the back room is wormy.
> Its meat is all stinky and squirmy,
> So I'm reading a book
> About how to cook
> And another about taxidermy.

In serious poetry most rhymes are monosyllabic (like *book* and *cook*), but **disyllabic rhymes** or **feminine rhymes** (those involving two syllables, like *wormy, squirmy,* and *taxidermy*) are often used, too. By "serious poetry," incidentally, I do not mean only that which is solemn in tone. Some serious poetry is quite funny, but there is a difference between it and comic poetry, which contains a lot of verbal clowning. Disyllabic rhymes tend to have a lightening, or ironic effect; they involve just a bit more wit than do monosyllabic rhymes and are a bit more noticeable. But the wit and irony can be quite poignant and moving, as in Edwin Arlington Robinson's "Eros Turannos" (the title means "Love, the Tyrant"). Here is the first stanza:

> She fears him, and will always ask
> > What fated her to choose him;
> She meets in his engaging mask
> > All reasons to refuse him;
> But what she meets and what she fears
> Are less than are the downward years,
> Drawn slowly to the foamless weirs
> > Of age, were she to lose him.

Masculine and feminine (or monosyllabic and disyllabic) rhymes alternate in the first four lines, then comes a series of three masculine rhymes, followed by a return to the feminine rhyme introduced before. Robinson, with such cleverness, is skirting the very edge of comedy as he depicts a situation of tragic love. Because the masculine rhymes are less obtrusive, less self-consciously clever, they help subdue the effect of the feminine rhymes by interrupting the sequence.

These particular feminine rhymes are even more noticeable than usual because they are **mosaic rhymes,** those in which the rhyme is made up of more than one word. The oft-quoted "shortest poem in the world," called "Fleas," is a mosaic rhyme: "Adam / Had 'em." Robert Browning was fond of mosaic rhymes, and in one serious poem used such pairs as these: *fabric/dab brick; far gain/bargain; all meant/installment; failure/pale lure; soon hit/unit; loosened/dew send.* Obviously these verge on the comic. When Robinson rhymes *choose him* with *refuse him,* the effect is lighter than, later in the same poem, such feminine rhymes as *confusion/illusion* or *given/driven.* Good poets invent challenges for themselves. In this case Robinson seems to have set for himself the problem of using feminine (including mosaic) rhymes for quiet irony without letting them disrupt the tone with comedy.

Much of your effort in rhyming is to subdue it. Intervening lines (such as the masculine rhymes in the stanza of Robinson's) have this effect. If you want to use a rhyme that is questionable, don't slap it right into a reader's face—unless you want him to laugh:

> My feet are wet, but there's no lack
> Of clean, dry socks in my knapsack.

The problem here is the primary stress on *knap*. Like many words in English, *knapsack* takes a stress on both syllables (otherwise it would sound something like *knapsik*), but the primary stress is on the first. Such words can be used as good rhymes, but you have to do it carefully. For one thing, if you have a doubtful rhyme, put it first of a rhyming pair; don't arrive at it as a climax. Another approach to a word such as *knapsack* is to precede it with a pyrrhic, so *knapsack* tends to be read as a spondee (or the two feet in combination as an Ionic: see Chapter 5). Break up the couplet with an intervening line. Is this better?

> Carry dry socks in a knapsack
>   And never mind the weather;
> Make up for sun that you may lack
>   By cushioning wet leather.

Now, as compared with the couplet given earlier, many elements are drawing attention away from the rhyme on *knapsack*—including the pyrrhic *in a* (much weaker than *in my*), which throws more stress onto the last syllable of *knapsack;* the placement of the word in the first rather than second position of the rhyme pair; and the shift of emphasis to the feminine rhyme of *weather* and *leather*.

A good poet can defy all these strictures, such as the one against identicals, while an unskilled poet might come up with an abomination such as:

> He had a brusque and haughty air
> Befitting for a son and heir
> Who wanted all to know his dad
> Was Calypso King of Trinidad.

But Robert Frost can use a blatant identical to make one of the most haunting couplets in our poetry:

> And miles to go before I sleep,
> And miles to go before I sleep.

He wrote the poem ("Stopping by Woods on a Snowy Evening") with an interlocking rhyme scheme, *a a b a, b b c b, c c d c* . . . (one line of each stanza interlocks with rhymes of the next). Then what? How was he going to end it? Boldly: *d d d d!* And, as though to make his point even more obvious, he repeated the whole line. In the quatrain above, *air/heir* and *dad/dad* look like accidents, as though the poet were unaware of the identicals or trying to cover them up. Better to shape them with clear artistic intent.

I call a rhyme such as *lack/knapsack* a **discordant rhyme,** and a rhyme such as *wall/animal* a **weak rhyme.** There is a discernible, or at least possible, stress on the last syllable of *animal,* but a primary stress on the second syllable of *knapsack* requires a distortion or mispronunciation. Discordant or weak rhymes are not necessarily bad rhymes. In fact, great poets such as Shakespeare or Browning are more likely to use them than are some of their less skilled contemporaries. Let's study the rhymes in one of the great poems of our language, "Sailing to Byzantium," by William Butler Yeats. Ancient Byzantium figured in Yeats's imagination as a kind of aesthetic ideal, a civilization of extreme artifice embodied especially in mosaics. In the first stanza he is rejecting his home country, Ireland:

> That is no country for old men. The young
> In one another's arms, birds in the trees
> —Those dying generations—at their song,
> The salmon-falls, the mackerel-crowded seas,
> Fish, flesh, or fowl, commend all summer long
> Whatever is begotten, born, and dies.
> Caught in that sensual music all neglect
> Monuments of unaging intellect.

Young is an off-rhyme with *song* and *long,* perhaps too close for comfort, but it is subdued by the enjambment of the first line and by separation by intervening lines. *Dies* is also an off-rhyme, distinct enough from *seas* and *trees* that it clearly does not seem a near-miss. It is used climactically, at the end of the sequence, and, moreover, the end of a sentence. *Intellect* is a weak rhyme for *neglect,* again used climactically, second of the pair, at the end of sentence and stanza, and in a couplet (without the softening effect of intervening lines). Each of the four stanzas ends with such a weak rhyme in a couplet. There is a reason for this. The couplets look deliberately artificial, forced. The poem is about the superiority of artifice to nature. The country he is leaving is dominated by the young who celebrate mortality—"Whatever is begotten, born, and dies." As

"An aged man" he wishes to be delivered from that mortal round:

> An aged man is but a paltry thing,
> A tattered coat upon a stick, unless
> Soul clap its hands and sing, and louder sing
> For every tatter in its mortal dress,
> Nor is there singing school but studying
> Monuments of its own magnificence;
> And therefore I have sailed the seas and come
> To the holy city of Byzantium.

Again the sequences of rhyme include weak rhymes and off-rhymes: *thing/sing/studying* and *unless/dress/magnificence*. We might associate the satisfying sonority of true rhymes with "that sensual music" from which he wants to be released, and the varieties of strained rhymes upon which he puts such emphasis as the song of the soul or intellect to which he aspires, the hard mosaic as opposed to a sensuous canvas.

In the third stanza he uses an idiosyncratic phrase, "perne in a gyre," meaning something like "spiral like a hawk," of special meaning to him, but the general intent is clear:

> O sages standing in God's holy fire
> As in the gold mosaic of a wall,
> Come from the holy fire, perne in a gyre,
> And be the singing-masters of my soul.
> Consume my heart away; sick with desire
> And fastened to a dying animal
> It knows not what it is; and gather me
> Into the artifice of eternity.

One sequence here is of true rhymes: *fire/gyre/desire*. But the other, including an off-rhyme and weak rhyme, is more climactic and striking: *wall/soul/animal*. It is that word *animal* which seems most uncannily powerful to me. I have not heard Yeats read this poem, though I have heard him read a number of his poems on records, and I know he almost crooned, eliciting the most from his meter and rhyme. I can imagine he would almost bawl *animal,* drawing out the last syllable in its forced rhyming with the distant *wall*. It culminates his rejection of flesh—that aging beast to which his heart is fastened.

Rhymes, like the ends of lines, stanzas, and strophes, can be used for the effect either of closure or of runover (or enjambment). When they coincide with the close of a rhetorical unit—a phrase or sentence—they are strong and emphatic, underscoring the structure of the poem. In Yeats's poem the stanzas are built of six-line units (with an alternating rhyme scheme *a b a b a b*), then a couplet. The first two stanzas have closure, emphasized by the rhyme, at the end of the six lines, setting the couplet off as a separate unit of thought. In the third the sense spills over into the couplet, without even a comma after *animal,* though one would help the clarity of the sentence, so eager the poet seems to be gathered up "into the artifice of eternity."

Eternity is out of nature, out of the biological world. Yeats concludes:

> Once out of nature I shall never take
> My bodily form from any natural thing,
> But such a form as Grecian goldsmiths make
> Of hammered gold and gold enamelling
> To keep a drowsy emperor awake;
> Or set upon a golden bough to sing
> To lords and ladies of Byzantium
> Of what is past, or passing, or to come.

The last three phrases are the eternal counterpart of mortality, of "Whatever is begotten, born, and dies." The rhymes in this stanza are all true, though two (*enamelling* and *Byzantium*) are weak. Notice that when *Byzantium* was used as a rhyme in the second stanza, it was in the climactic second position. Here it is subdued by being used first, allowing the poem to close on the strong *come.*

Rhyme, of course, is a minor aspect of the greatness of this poem, but yet is subtly relevant to its majestic theme. Yeats probably managed it with brilliant intuition rather than conscious planning. *Mosaic,* deriving ultimately from the Latin and Greek words for muse, means a work of art made up of tiny pieces fitted intricately together. The rhymes here are tiles in a mosaic of eternity.

You see places where Yeats has pushed artificialities to the fore for deliberate emphasis and places where he has used them for unobtrusive resonance. Most often poets seek unobtrusiveness. The reader may not be conscious of the rhyme at all, and yet syllables and words linger in the ear as distant overtones.

There are many fewer rhymes available in English than in most other modern languages. The Romance languages, especially, tend to have vast numbers of words with similar endings. Rhyme in English, therefore, is somewhat more ingenious—and attracts more attention to itself—than in other languages. If readers become too conscious of rhyme, the poem seems to jingle. Consequently, much of the technique for good rhyming is involved in tucking it away until there is occasion for emphasis.

When you read amateur rhymed poetry you can almost hear each line come panting up to its rhyme like a local subway to its frequent stops. In Chapter 5 we saw how Pope made most of his lines and couplets come to end-stops, emphasizing the rhyme as the completion of a unit of thought. Here is Robert Browning using the same form, rhymed iambic pentameter couplets:

> That's my last Duchess painted on the wall,
> Looking as if she were alive. I call
> That piece a wonder, now: Frá Pandolf's hands
> Worked busily a day, and there she stands.

The sharp enjambment and late caesura in the second line suppress the word to be rhymed. The third line is also enjambed, so the first place that a rhetorical stop corresponds to the end of the sentence becomes a moment of minor climax. Study this technique in the remainder of the poem, "My Last Duchess," which is commonly anthologized. Many hear the entire poem without realizing that it is rhymed. But the rhymes have nonetheless a powerful effect at those moments of climax and otherwise are held like a sheathed sword, at the ready though restrained.

Avoid rare words in rhyming positions, unless, again, you want to be comic. Many of the words you find in rhyming dictionaries are useless to you in serious poetry. Could you include in a poem such rhymes as *dichroic, melanchroic, pleochroic, xanthochroic, dypnoic, troic, azoic, benzoic, Cenozoic, Eozoic, hylozoic, hypnozoic, Mezozoic?* Just try one:

> Muhammad Ali proved himself heroic.
> By being proud he wasn't xanthochroic.

It looks like what it is—an effort to get that rare word (which means "pertaining to white persons with light hair and fair skin") into a rhyme.

That's clowning, wrenching meaning to draw attention to rhyme for its own sake. If for some strange reason you wanted to use such a word as that, bury it in the line:

> Defiantly Muhammad Ali hurled
> Himself into the xanthochroic world.

Much of your work with rhyme will be rewriting to get those words into rhyme position which offer some possibility of good poetry. If you wrote a line ending with *heroic,* then went searching for a rhyme, you would find there is really only one good possibility, *stoic.* These two words are somewhat associated in meaning. Rhyming them would make it look as though, having gotten *heroic* in (and being too lazy to rewrite), you were forced to work in *stoic.* Rewrite. Get some other word at the end of the line, one with more rhyme possibilities.

Except in unusual cases, you won't want your rhymes to stick out like sore thumbs. Avoid awkward inversions, expletives, artificial contractions, and other devices which poets have often used, lazily, to make their rhymes come out right. I will illustrate:

> When you your words do rearrange
> And seem reluctant them to change
> And sprinkle *'tis*'s, *ere*'s and *e'er*'s
> To smooth your meter, chime your pairs,
> Such faults are not exactly sin—
> But grate, like a squeaky violin.

In the first line, *do* is an expletive, a word unnecessary for meaning, put in as metrical padding. Both the first two lines have awkward inversions, distortions of idiomatic word order. Some inversions are very effective, but these are terrible, and obviously used only to get words into rhyme positions. The contractions in the third line (*'tis* and *e'er* for *it is* and *ever*) are sure giveaways of amateur poetry; they are never used *except* in poetry, and, today, except in bad poetry. *Ere* is a perfectly good word, but archaic, and it has come to be a cliché in amateur poetry.

Listen to your own speech. You should be able to pronounce rhyming words naturally, comfortably; if they feel forced to you, they will seem so to a reader. On the other hand, don't slouch, as most of us do in ordinary conversation. Give each syllable its full value. Unless you are deliberately writing dialect verse (indicated by unconventional spelling and punctuation), it is best to adhere to the standard pronunciations indicated by contemporary American dictionaries. This standard is sometimes called "broadcast American." (Its English equivalent is called "BBC English.") Electronic communication has to a great extent ironed out regional differences in our speech. If you rhyme *rather* with *father* instead of with *lather* in your daily speech, fine, but if you put that rhyme into a poem you should know it is, nationally, a secondary pronunciation and will seem to many readers an affectation. If you say "Berl the boid in erl" for what is usually spelled "Boil the bird in oil," there is nothing wrong with your speech; but if you rhyme *bird* with *void* in your poem, the effect may be comic, or, at best, perceived as an off-rhyme.

If you approach rhyming with the attitude of one trying to get away with minimal effort, you would be better off to avoid rhyme (and perhaps avoid writing poetry) altogether. I get many communications each year from poets complaining that editors will not take rhymed, metrical poetry, that there is a prejudice against "traditional" verse. I am inclined to agree that there is such a bias in intellectual circles, but when I see the work of those who complain, I know it was rejected, not because it was rhymed and metrical, but because it was just plain bad writing. Moreover, when I look at anthologies of good modern poetry I find that most of it is metrical, much of it rhymed. This is also increasingly true in literary journals. Even some of the poets of the Beat generation of the fifties are now writing metrical, rhymed poetry.

Much poor writing gets by as free verse. Ineptitudes or obscurities may be attributed to creativity by editors of generous mind. But sloppiness shows up more quickly in rhymed verse. Some poets seem to think that if they can just get lines to rhyme, their job is done. The truth is quite the opposite. Rhyme has such a powerful effect in poetry that it immediately stands out when awkwardly used. Use it with caution and caring, toning it down, smoothing it over, keeping it from embarrassing you like a show-off child.

9

Yard Goods

Verse Paragraphs, Stanzas, Strophes

The texture of poetry is woven of word choices, rhythms, line breaks, sounds, and rhymes, such as we have studied in earlier chapters. Here we will consider the yard goods: the larger units of which whole poems are made. We have yet to deal with the structure of finished articles and should remember that many can write poetry, often very good poetry, by the yard, but few are successful in making finished poems.

As mentioned in Chapter 1, there are three basic **genres** of poetry: **narrative, dramatic,** and **lyric.** A narrative tells a story. A piece of dramatic poetry usually tells a story, too, but it dramatizes the action, with fictional characters speaking the lines. The term *lyric* comes from the word for a musical instrument, the lyre, and it once meant poetry to be sung. However, the meaning has been so broadened in the course of history that now lyrics can be best defined by negatives: they are poems, usually short, which are *not* narrative or dramatic. The genres are often blended with one another. A **ballad,** or story poem to be sung, is a lyrical narrative. Plays such as those of Shakespeare often have songs, or lyrics, introduced into them, or rhapsodic passages—such as Romeo's praise of Juliet before she knows he is in her garden—that are lyrical in tone. Ancient Greek drama was punctuated by choral passages which were lyrical comments on or meditations about the action. Sometimes characters (especially, in Greek drama, messengers) recount offstage action in vivid, extended speeches—little narratives in the midst of the drama. Sometimes lyrics are written in the "voice" of a fictional character, such as a **dramatic monologue** such as Browning's "My Last Duchess," which is spoken by a duke. Many modern poets use a **persona,** or "mask" or assumed character, as the speaker in their poems, even when the poems seem to be in the poet's own voice. Indeed, some modern critics have suggested that we consider all lyrics as though each were a speech from a play, for though the poet might have intended to speak frankly in his or her own voice, the poet changes in mood and circumstances, so the speaker in the poem is, in effect, a fictional creation. That approach completely absorbs the lyric in the dramatic genre.

Probably the bulk of the world's poetry—ancient and modern, but especially modern—is lyrical, though the long epics and other narratives and vast literature of poetic drama may, combined, equal in number of lines the amount of lyrical poetry. Nonetheless, when most people say "a poem," they probably are not thinking of a narrative or dramatic poem but of a lyric. In this era of printing, most poems are written to be read, so the connection with song has become very distant. However, it might be said that lyrics begin in an emotional, or at least a subjective, response of a speaker (or singer) to experience. Most lyrics are written in the first person. They are subjective rather than objective—that is, they emphasize the personal, the individual response, rather than attempt to report objective truth. Many of the most ancient lyrics have religious or even mystical functions. They may mourn the dead, praise the gods or great heroes or important public occasions, celebrate births, marriages, historic events. **Mystical poems** are those inspired by direct (real or imagined) personal experience with the supernatural. These may be oracular, like the visions of the prophets. (For a modern example, see W. B. Yeats's "The Second Coming.") Or they may express a saint's (or someone else's) personal experience of God, often in quite erotic terms. Sometimes they attack social evils, often by ridicule, and are called **satires.** Sometimes they teach morals, the good life, or convey bodies of factual knowledge. These are called **didactic poems.** Before you can decide on a form for your poem, you need to know what kind of poem it will be. Consideration of these and other possibilities will increase your range.

Within the poem there are generally units which are larger than the individual lines, but smaller than the whole poem. The principal varieties of such units are **verse paragraphs, stanzas,** and **strophes.** Long narratives and didactic, or essaylike, poems usually have verse paragraphs, which, like prose paragraphs, are unified by content. In Chapter 5 we studied a few lines of Alexander Pope's "An Essay on Criticism." As the title implies, his purpose was didactic. He wanted to teach his readers how to write and evaluate poetry. It goes on for many pages, but when he changes from one subject to another, he indents, starting a new verse paragraph. When, in narrative, one speaker is interrupted by another, the poet usually, like an author of prose, starts a new verse paragraph. This may be indicated by a mid-line drop, or by an indentation, or sometimes by a space on the page. Here is a passage from Robert Frost's "Home Burial":

> "Amy! Don't go to someone else this time.
> Listen to me. I won't come down the stairs."
> He sat and fixed his chin between his fists.
> "There's something I should like to ask you, dear."
>
> "You don't know how to ask it."
>   "Help me, then."
>
> Her fingers moved the latch for all reply.
>
> "My words are nearly always an offense."

The husband is speaking in the first of these verse paragraphs. Then his action is described, then he speaks again—all in the same verse paragraph. The space indicates a new verse paragraph and change of speaker. We know it is the wife responding. The dropped line introduces a new verse paragraph, and the husband again. Since the next action is hers, not his, it is set off in a one-line verse paragraph.

Often you find the words *stanza* and *strophe* used interchangeably, but I will distinguish between them. A stanza is more like a box—a fixed shape into which you fit the contents. A strophe is more like a bag which adapts itself to the shape of the contents. Stanzas resemble metrical verse in that they impose (to some degree) a measure or order on the language. Strophes resemble free verse: their length and form are freely varied to suit the poet's needs and intentions.

Stanza comes from an Italian word meaning station, or stopping place—ultimately from the Latin verb for stand. It usually has a fixed form. That is, the corresponding lines of each stanza of a poem will be in the same meter and will rhyme (if they rhyme at all) in the same pattern. For example, Percy Bysshe Shelley's "To a Skylark" has 21 stanzas, all following the pattern of the first:

> Hail to thee, blithe spirit!
> Bird thou never wert—
> That from heaven or near it
> Pourest thy full heart
> In profuse strains of unpremeditated art.

The first and third lines rhyme, and we call that rhyme *a*. The second, fourth, and fifth lines rhyme (in this case with an off-rhyme), and we call that rhyme *b*. The first four lines each have three feet; the fifth has six. The scheme for the stanza (see Chapter 5) can thus be indicated as $a^3 b^3 a^3 b^3 b^6$, with the further note that lines 1-4 are trochaic (or headless iambic) and line 5 is iambic.

I don't know that Shelley or any other poet ever used that particular stanza pattern in any other poem. Many stanza patterns are invented for a specific poem. Others have become traditional and have been used again and again. Perhaps the most familiar is the ballad stanza, which we have discussed in Chapter 5—the form of "Mary had a little lamb," or "Yankee Doodle," and of many of the poems of Emily Dickinson. Can you write the formula for a ballad stanza on the basis of these familiar examples? Here is a stanza from "Sir Patrick Spens," a traditional folk ballad:

> The king sits in Dumferling toune,
> Drinking the blude-reid wine:
> "O whar will I get guid sailor,
> To sail this schip of mine?"

The meter is rough, especially when it impels us to say *sail-OR,* but I think you can make it out: iambic, $x^4 a^3 x^4 a^3$ (the *x*'s indicate lines that do not rhyme). Not all folk ballads follow this pattern, but enough do that it has come to be recognized as the **ballad stanza**. Here is an exception, from another ballad, "Edward":

> "Why dois your brand sae drap wi bluid,
>   Edward, Edward,
> Why dois your brand sae drap wi bluid,
>   And why sae sad gang yee O?"
> "O I hae killed my hauke sae guid,
>   Mither, mither,
> O I hae killed my hauke sae guid,
>   And I had nae mair but hee O."

In this stanza pattern whole lines are repeated, and the repeated *O* must be read as a monosyllabic foot. If you have ever heard this tragic and gruesome ballad sung by a rich bass voice, you know the power of the repetitions and identicals in building suspense, lamentation, and horror.

Stanzas, like lines, can be open or enjambed. That is, the end of the stanza need not coincide with a rhetorical pause or completion of an idea. Dante invented a form of interlocking stanzas for *The Divine Comedy* which has come to be called **terza rima.** See if you can work out its formula from this example by W. H. Auden (from "The Sea and the Mirror"):

> As all the pigs have turned back into men
> And the sky is auspicious and the sea
> Calm as a clock, we can all go home again.
>
> Yes, it undoubtedly looks as if we
> Could take life as easily now as tales
> Write ever-after: not only are the
>
> Two heads silhouetted against the sails
> —And kissing, of course—well-built, but the lean
> Fool is quite a person, the fingernails
>
> Of the dear old butler for once quite clean,
> And the royal passengers quite as good
> As rustics, perhaps better, for they mean
>
> What they say. . . . .

Auden plays fast and loose with his trochees and pyrrhics, but you should be able to find five feet in each line. The *terza rima* rhyme pattern has been used with lines of various lengths, however. Did you get it? It goes *a b a, b c b, c d c,* and so forth, the middle line of one stanza providing the rhyme for the first and third of the next. Clearly the pattern can be extended indefinitely. Sometimes poets end it with a single line, set off, rounding off the rhyme from the middle of the final stanza: *y z y, z.* Notice the enjambment of *the/Two* between the second and third stanzas above.

Shelley took *terza rima* one step further in the stanza pattern of his "Ode to the West Wind." The poem is made up of five units, numbered, each following the formula of this first one:

> O wild West Wind, thou breath of Autumn's being,
> Thou, from whose unseen presence the leaves dead
> Are driven, like ghosts from an enchanter fleeing,
>
> Yellow, and black, and pale, and hectic red,
> Pestilence-stricken multitudes: O thou,
> Who chariotest to their dark wintry bed
>
> The wingèd seeds, where they die cold and low,
> Each like a corpse within its grave, until
> Thine azure sister of the spring shall blow
>
> Her clarion o'er the dreaming earth, and fill
> (Driving sweet buds like flocks to feed in air)
> With living hues and odours plain and hill;
>
> Wild Spirit, which art moving everywhere;
> Destroyer and preserver; hear, O hear!

The whole group of fourteen lines (a variation on the sonnet) is a stanza. Within it are four *terza rima* units, concluded by a couplet that finishes off the rhyme from the middle of the last such unit.

You will find references to other stanza forms which have been widely used in the past (for example, **ottava rima:** iambic *a b a b a b c c;* **rhyme royal:** iambic pentameter, *a b a b b c c;* **Spenserian:** iambic *a b a b- b c b c c,* the first eight lines being pentameter, the last hexameter). You may find these useful, or, perhaps, you will do best to invent your own.

In good stanzaic poetry there is a tension between the expectations created by the form and the pull of the narrative or argument or emotional development. In modern poetry the trend is away from the elaborate and rather long stanzas of the past. A stanzaic pattern may be as simple as a couplet, triplet, or quatrain, perhaps with a rhyme somewhere, perhaps not. Those of Robert Lowell in "Skunk Hour" consist of six lines (of various lengths) with at least one rhyme or off-rhyme and perhaps more to the stanza. Here are the third through fifth stanzas:

> The season's ill—
> we've lost our summer millionaire,
> who seemed to leap from an L. L. Bean
> catalogue. His nine-knot yawl
> was auctioned off to lobstermen.
> A red fox stain covers Blue Hill.
>
> And now our fairy
> decorator brightens his shop for fall;
> his fishnet's filled with orange cork,
> orange, his cobbler's bench and awl;
> there is no money in his work,
> he'd rather marry.
>
> One dark night,
> my Tudor Ford climbed the hill's skull:
> I watched for love-cars. Lights turned down,
> they lay together, hull to hull,
> where the graveyard shelves on the town. . . .
> My mind's not right.

There is a subtle linking between stanzas by the rhymes of the fourth lines here (and in some other stanzas)—*yawl, awl, hull,* reinforced by *skull, fall, ill, Hill.* The first and last lines of these (and some other) stanzas rhyme. But no pattern is consistent. The looseness is appropriate to the sequence of casual observations, some satirical, of the island and of the poet, who says "I myself am hell" and identifies with a family of skunks, a mother leading her three kittens up Main Street, under the spire of the Trinitarian Church, to swill garbage—"and will not scare." As in all stanzaic poetry, it is the interplay of the more or less rigid form with the content that keeps the poem tense and moving.

Strophe comes from the Greek word for turning (as *verse* comes from the Latin word for turning). Originally it referred to the first part of the chorus in Greek drama. The actors would speak the lines of the strophe while moving across the stage in one direction, then those of the **anti-strophe** as they returned, then those of the **epode** while standing still. (The strophe and antistrophe would be in the same metrical form, the epode in a different one.) Thus the strophe is associated with movement and emotion, self-expression. It does not have the narrative or logical cohesion of a verse paragraph, nor the strictly repeated form of a stanza. William Wordsworth's "Ode: Intimations of Immortality from Recollections of Early Childhood" is written in strophes, of which these are the first two:

1

There was a time when meadow, grove, and stream
    The earth, and every common sight,
            To me did seem
        Appareled in celestial light,
The glory and the freshness of a dream.
It is not now as it hath been of yore;—
            Turn whereso'er I may,
                By night or day,
The things which I have seen I now can see no more.

2

        The rainbow comes and goes,
        And lovely is the rose,
        The moon doth with delight
Look round her when the heavens are bare,
        Waters on a starry night
        Are beautiful and fair;
        The sunshine is a glorious birth;
        But yet I know, where'er I go,
That there hath passed away a glory from the earth.

The implication of a strophe is that the poet is somehow moved to break off and start a new unit. These strophes are unified in content, like verse paragraphs, but the various line lengths and rhyme patterns suggest emotional demands too strong to be contained in a preconceived format.

In "Ode to the Confederate Dead" Allen Tate wanted to convey the drifting thought of a person in a graveyard contemplating the meaning of death and of the Confederate struggle. Indentations, spaces, and dropped lines are signals of strophic turnings required by shifts of thought and emotion, very different from the kind of rhetorical unity we associate with verse paragraphs. These lines are from the middle of the poem:

> Turn your eyes to the immoderate past,
> Turn to the inscrutable infantry rising
> Demons out of the earth—they will not last.
> Stonewall, Stonewall, and the sunken fields of hemp,
> Shiloh, Antietam, Malvern Hill, Bull Run.
> Lost in that orient of the thick-and-fast
> You will cure the setting sun.
>
>   Cursing only the leaves crying
>   Like an old man in a storm
>
> You hear the shout, the crazy hemlocks point
> With troubled fingers to the silence which
> Smothers you, a mummy, in time.
>
>   The hound bitch
> Toothless and dying, in a musty cellar
> Hears the wind only.
>
>   Now that the salt of their blood
> Stiffens the saltier oblivion of the sea, . . .

These strophes are closed, more or less unified in content. But other modern poets often used enjambed strophes and abrupt shifts and arbitrary spacing to generate tension and, perhaps, to imitate the darting of the mind. Here are some lines from William Carlos Williams's *Paterson,* Book V:

> Her
>   hips were narrow, her
>   legs
> thin and straight She stopped

me in my tracks—until I saw
her
　　　disappear in the crowd.

It is not always possible to find a rationale for the way free-verse poems are broken into units, any more than it is to know why the lines are divided as they are. The poet felt like doing it that way, and that seems to be reason enough.

But if you look hard enough, you can usually find the reasons for the formal arrangements used by most good poets. Such whimsy in both form and content as seen in these lines from Paul Blackburn's "The Watchers" will no doubt soon be forgotten (if ever noted) by readers of poetry:

earth / debris / & schist, the stud/stuff of the island
　　　is moved by this
　　　PASCO
　　　CAT-933
　　　ORegon 6-
it does not rain • smoke, the
　　　　　　　alpha-beta-tau

raised from　5 vowels,　13 consonants to
　　　　　　5 vowels,　15 consonants
　　　　　　(Epicharmus) not
the Sicilian writer of comedies, 6 A.D., but
his ancestor /
the Aesculapius family at Cos, a couple are . . .

And so on. It doesn't much matter where you start or stop.

Unfortunately, so much poetry is published which has random and arbitrary form that readers become dulled to the subtleties in a poem such as Richard Wilbur's "Love Calls Us to the Things of This World":

　　The eyes open to a cry of pulleys,
And spirited from sleep, the astounded soul
Hangs for a moment bodiless and simple
As false dawn.

Outside the open window
The morning air is all awash with angels.

Some are in bed-sheets, some are in blouses,
Some are in smocks: but truly there they are.
Now they are rising together in calm swells
Of halcyon feeling, filling whatever they wear
With the deep joy of their impersonal breathing;

Now they are flying in place, conveying
The terrible speed of their omnipresence, moving
And staying like white water, and now of a sudden
They swoon down into so rapt a quiet
That nobody seems to be there.
The soul shrinks

From all that it is about to remember,
From the punctual rape of every blessed day,
And cries,
"Oh, let there be nothing on earth but laundry,
Nothing but rosy hands in the rising steam
And clear dances done in the sight of heaven."

Yet, as the sun acknowledges
With a warm look the world's hunks and colors,
The soul descends once more in bitter love
To accept the waking body, saying now
In a changed voice as the man yawns and rises,

"Bring them down from their ruddy gallows;
Let there be clean linen for the backs of thieves;
Let lovers go fresh and sweet to be undone,
And the heaviest nuns walk in a pure floating
Of dark habits,
keeping their difficult balance."

First, notice that the poem is built of six unrhymed, five-line stanzas. Each starts with an indented line. That makes them look like verse paragraphs, but, actually, the indentation is for another reason. Can you find it? If you scan the poem you will discover that the first line of each stanza has only four feet, the other lines having five. The first lines are indented because they are shorter.

Thus the poem has a stanzaic pattern. But what about the dropped lines? These are often, in poetry, indications of new verse paragraphs; and, if we look, we find that, indeed, a pattern of verse paragraphs is superimposed on the stanzaic pattern. The first paragraph goes down to "false dawn." There is then a change of subject, and a new paragraph. It extends past the end of the first stanza, through the second stanza, clear down to the last line of the third, where there is another drop. The first paragraph described the man waking, before he was fully in touch with reality. The second describes his hallucination, that angels are flying outside his window—and ends with "nobody seems to be there." The description, from "awash" on, is given in such a way that we know the man sees only laundry flapping on the line, but the language is filled with the visionary delight he must experience, seeing all those angels—and with humor, too, as he imagines with what "terrible speed" angels must have to travel always to be everywhere at once.

"The soul shrinks" begins a new paragraph. The man has now grasped that he is looking at laundry, is delighted, and reflects on the experience. There is another dropped line when he begins to speak, setting the remainder of stanza 4 off in a paragraph by itself. The hinge of the poem is the word "Yet," occurring where a paragraph and stanza (with its indentation) begin together. It's time to get up, to put the soul back into the body, to take the laundry off the line. It is with "bitter love" that the man accepts his body, the "world's hunks and colors," but it is a comfortable love, too, as he becomes reoriented to fact and function. And look what has happened to the form! The tension between the stanzaic and paragraph structure seems to be resolved. Stanzas 5 and 6 are complete verse paragraphs within themselves, their indentations serving as paragraph indentations—until the last line.

What happens there? Surely not another verse paragraph! Well, he has said the linen is for thieves and lovers and nuns, the last being committed to things not of this world. Their floating is pure, but their habits are dark (double pun!). They, like the suspended soul at the beginning of the poem, are half-removed from reality, maintaining a difficult balance between soul and world. The broken line tips us again off balance, from a state of firm resolution *into* a difficult balance. The isolated phrase at the end is like a response to the whole poem. It is an insistence on angels *and* laundry. It is a lyric turning, a choral commentary, a little bit of a strophe overlaid on the structure of verse paragraphs overlaid on stanzas!

The poem is worth study in detail, for it suggests the range of possibilities you have in designing your own poems. Try each. I suggest you start with a short narrative, paragraphing as you would in writing fiction to indicate changes in subject or mood, changes in speakers, shifts of time. Then, with that poem or another, count the total number of lines and find out by what factors they are divisible. For instance, a thirty-six-line poem might have six units of six lines, three units of twelve lines, twelve units of three lines, eighteen units of two lines, two units of eighteen lines. Try each. Does any rewriting suggest itself that would make these units more effective as stanzas?

I often make pencil marks in the margin of a poem to indicate different units before deciding on a final shape. These help me visualize how the poem would look in various forms. Of course one has to rewrite afterwards, adapting the poem to the form chosen, or start from the beginning with a form in mind, taking advantage of the breaks, shaping the content to fit. The paragraph breaks are rhetorical, organically related to meaning. The stanza breaks, arrived at by arbitrary division into units of equal lines, are deliberately, consciously formal. Do they do anything interesting to the poem? Do you find some stanzas enjambed in significant ways, some happening on appropriate (but perhaps surprising) moments of closure?

Now look at the poem a third way, in terms of strophes. Ignore the logical or rhetorical divisions and the arbitrary divisions arrived at by line count. Look, rather, for instances of dramatic pause, of turning. These may be related to sound echoes or other elements as well as to emotional development. Look for patterns in your poem you might not have been aware of, patterns you might bring out or heighten by sensitive grouping of lines. It is now the total aesthetic impact of the poem you are considering. What are you bringing attention to? What are you strategically suppressing?

Remember that the satisfactions provided by structure are many and varied and sometimes contradictory. Paragraphing reinforces meaning, making your poem easier to understand and to think about. That may be a primary value for you, but you should remember what we have learned about phrasal (or rhetorical) line breaks. They can be dull. If you use a line ending or a paragraph break to do a job that sensitive reading achieves without it, you are, in effect, wasting a resource. For instance, if it is perfectly obvious that you have changed subjects, do you really need a paragraph break to signal the change? Use the break for something else, something which might otherwise be lost without your artful spacing. Remember the pleasure the reader may find in putting things together, seeing connections you have not blatantly pointed to. Remember also the dangers of overdoing it, of making your poem obscure by blurring its logical divisions, or of seeming flamboyant in your self-conscious manipulation of words on the page.

How much should you be concerned with visual symmetry? That is, of course, a matter of taste. Are you writing the poem primarily to be looked at or to be heard? Are you being merely cute or busy or ingenious in making visual arrangements, or do these have something to do with your larger purposes in this poem (or in poetry in general)? Are you helping a performer by providing a good script for dramatic reading? Or are you deliberately arranging your lines to play against the demands of performance? Why? There can be genuine aesthetic advantages to either approach, or in some mixture of the two.

To illustrate, I will arbitrarily divide a short poem in three ways, and tell you later who wrote it and how it was divided by the poet. It is entitled "A Sort of Song":

> Let the snake wait under
> his weed
> and the writing
>
> be of words, slow and quick, sharp
> to strike, quiet to wait,
> sleepless.
>
> —through metaphor to reconcile
> the people and the stones.
> Compose. (No ideas

but in things) Invent!
Saxifrage is my flower that splits
the rocks.

Let the snake wait under
his weed

and the writing
be of words, slow and quick, sharp
to strike, quiet to wait,
sleepless.
—through metaphor to reconcile
the people and the stones.

Compose.
                    (No ideas
but in things)   Invent!

Saxifrage is my flower that splits
the rocks.

Let the snake wait
                        under
his weed
and the writing
be
    of words, slow and quick, sharp
to strike,
                quiet to wait,
sleepless.
—through metaphor
                        to reconcile
the people and the stones.

```
Compose.   (No ideas
but
      in things)
                  Invent!
Saxifrage
         is my flower
                  that splits
the rocks.
```

The first version is arbitrarily broken into stanzas of three lines. Try it with four, with two, with six, and see how it feels. The second version is a kind of mixture of verse-paragraph structure and strophe structure, with greater unity in the parts than in the stanzaic structure. The poem doesn't lend itself very well to paragraph structure, but you might see if you can find a way of emphasizing its thought development and logical divisions better than this effort. The third, with its very short (sometimes one-word) strophes, uses spacing and mid-line breaks for dramatic emphasis. Those three-part lines, such as

```
Saxifrage
         is my flower
                  that splits
```

look a little like the work of William Carlos Williams, don't they? Well, actually, the poem is by William Carlos Williams, but he divided it simply into two stanzas of six lines each, the stanza break falling after "sleepless." Is any of these ways, his or mine, better than the others?

If you thought I was going to tell you the right way to write a poem, I hope you were disabused many chapters ago. I couldn't tell you if I knew, and if I knew for one poem, I wouldn't know for the next. All I can do is show you some of the things poets have done in the past, to good and bad effect, and help you ask yourself the questions that may lead you to original answers. Tradition is satisfying; so is innovation. It's your show.

10

The Shape of Human Thought

Fixed Forms; The Sonnet

We have considered the units within poems—verse paragraphs, stanzas, and strophes—but have not yet dealt with the structure of whole poems. It is, of course, difficult to generalize about how poems can be structured; they have infinite variety. But we can learn something about questions of overall structure by looking at some small examples, especially at the most common of the fixed forms, the sonnet.

When do you have not just poetry, but a poem? It is surprising how often in workshop discussions we discover in one another's work that two poems or more have gotten tangled together as one. Sometimes the confusion is one of imagery: for example, a mechanical way of thinking about life has intruded on an organic way, like a machine in the garden, and while either might make a good poem, their combination is merely confusing and distracting. Sometimes it is a narrative tangle. A woman starts to tell about something she has observed (or pretended to observe). In the process she has to tell something about herself (or the speaker in the poem)—for instance, why she happened to be there, what her relationship was to the persons observed. In the resulting poem we can see that she was really more interested in the first-person experience than in the experience observed. "That's your poem," we say. Shift the emphasis. Focus on the speaker. Take out most of the stuff about the people you were observing. Save that for another poem.

Or maybe both should be included, but the poem should simply be longer, fully developing both the experience of the observer and the experience observed, and making some coherent connection between them. Maybe there should be two poems as part of a series, each of which works on its own, both taking on greater significance when read in the context of the series. Constant tension between various kinds of unity and interrelationship generates power in most works of poetry, long or short.

The length of most poems is, of course, determined by content. Epics and some didactic poems run to book length. Poems may have any number of stanzas, strophes, or verse paragraphs. There are some poems, however, in which the overall length is predetermined. These are sometimes called the **fixed forms,** though, as we will see in regard to the sonnet, that, too, is a relative term. Some are more fixed than others. For example, the Japanese form **haiku** has become popular in the United States, probably because it seems so easy to write (though extremely difficult to write well). The Japanese form has a strict syllable count: the three lines have, respectively, five, seven, and five syllables. *Kigo,* or traditional terms for the seasons and natural elements, are used in a specific manner. There is a great deal more to the haiku tradition, involving a way of observing nature with Zen-like objectivity, but writers of haiku in English adapt the form to their own uses. Some strictly follow the syllable-count formula, others think any short poem in the spirit of the haiku is acceptable, such as Ezra Pound's:

In a Station of the Metro

The apparition of these faces in the crowd;
Petals on a wet, black bough.

Some carefully include a traditional kigo, or season word, translated from the Japanese, such as "misty moonlight," or "lingering daylight," or mention a kind of flower or animal observed in a certain season. Others ignore kigo altogether. The cult of American haiku writers is fiercely divided, quite in contrast to the delicacy of their little verses.

A similar, if less intense, cult writes what are called "Crapsey **cinquains**"—poems with lines of, respectively, two, four, six, eight, and two syllables. A *cinquain* is any five-line stanza or poem, but Adelaide

Crapsey, influenced by Japanese poetry, designed the specific formula for her volume of *Verses,* published, after her death, in 1915.

A poem of fixed form which is more native to our language is the **limerick,** considered briefly in Chapters 5 and 7, an ancient form of unknown origin appearing even in the Mother Goose rhymes (for example, "Hickory Dickory Dock"). It is generally anapestic, $a^3 a^3 b^2 b^2 a^3$, but the *b* lines are often iambic (for example, "the clock struck one / and down he run''). Limericks, which are almost always comic, are the only fixed-form poems I know of which originated in English. French and Italian poetry produced many fixed forms, often with complex rhyme schemes which are difficult to adapt to English because rhymes in our language are so much more scarce. Some have repeated whole lines, as in the **villanelle.** The best-known example of the villanelle in modern English is by Dylan Thomas:

> Do not go gentle into that good night,
> Old age should burn and rave at close of day;
> Rage, rage against the dying of the light.
>
> Though wise men at their end know dark is right,
> Because their words had forked no lightning they
> Do not go gentle into that good night.
>
> Good men, the last wave by, crying how bright
> Their frail deeds might have danced in a green bay,
> Rage, rage against the dying of the light.
>
> Wild men who caught and sang the sun in flight,
> And learn, too late, they grieved it on its way,
> Do not go gentle into that good night.
>
> Grave men, near death, who see with blinding sight
> Blind eyes could blaze like meteors and be gay,
> Rage, rage against the dying of the light.
>
> And you, my father, there on the sad height,
> Curse, bless, me now with your fierce tears, I pray.
> Do not go gentle into that good night.
> Rage, rage against the dying of the light.

Many villanelles are in tetrameter, but this one is pentameter. It is the rhyme scheme and pattern of repetition of the two key lines which determine the villanelle, and you can derive them from this example. The trick is to find two lines which can bear that much repetition and which change slightly in meaning as the poem develops.

Less frequently adapted to English is the **sestina.** The formula for this poem depends not on rhymes, but on the repetition of the words which end lines—in a very specific pattern. Here are the first two stanzas of Ezra Pound's "Sestina: Altaforte":

> Damn it all! all this our South stinks peace.
> You whoreson dog, Papiols, come! Let's to music!
> I have no life save when the swords clash.
> But ah! When I see the standards gold, vair, purple,
>   opposing,
> And the broad fields beneath them turn crimson,
> Then howl I my heart nigh mad with rejoicing.
>
> In hot summer have I great rejoicing
> When the tempests kill the earth's foul peace,
> And the lightnings from black heav'n flash crimson,
> And the fierce thunders roar me their music
> And the winds shriek through the clouds mad, opposing,
> And through all the riven skies God's swords clash.

Let's use capital letters for the final words—A for *peace,* B for *music,* and so on. There are six stanzas using these words in this pattern (of which you can see the first two stanzas above): *ABCDEF, FAEBDC, CFDABE, ECBFAD, DEACFB, BDFECA.* Then there is an **envoy,** ending with *ECA* or *ACE,* but B, D, and F may occur within the lines. Here is the envoy from Pound's poem:

> And let the music of the swords make them crimson!
> Hell grant soon we hear again the swords clash!
> Hell blot black for alway the thought "Peace"!

Sestinas tax one's ingenuity and tend to be tedious, but many excellent poets have tried their hand at the form.

But by far the most flexible and common poem of more or less fixed form is the **sonnet.** I have used examples of sonnets throughout the book to give you a sense of the range of the form. The sonnet form has become so universal in European and American culture since its invention in thirteenth-century Italy that it seems almost to be some mysterious embodiment of the shape of human thought. Studying it will help you understand that writing poetry is not a matter of following rules, for the fascination of the sonnet, like the fascination of meter, results from the strain of content against the form. Nothing is fixed. There are no rules. Yet there is enough consistency in the way poets return and return to the form that one can discern beneath the infinite variation some inalterable essence, "a something white, uncertain," one might say. I will come back to that quotation.

First I will run through the usuals. Sonnets in English are usually fourteen-line poems of iambic pentameter with a rhyme scheme that follows or varies in some recognizable way any of several traditional patterns. There are usually two discernible parts of the poem. A problem or experience is set up in the first eight lines (called the **octave**), and there is a response to it, or resolution, in the last six lines (called the **sestet**).

I say "the usuals" because there are well-known and recognized exceptions to each of them in sonnet literature. The Italian sonnet was given its final form by Dante and Petrarch (and is often called the Petrarchan sonnet). Its octave is made up of two quatrains rhyming *a b b a a b b a*. The sestet is more varied, usually consisting of two tercets with any of various rhyme patterns, such as *c d e c d e, c d c e d e, c d c d c d, c d c d c d*. (Notice the two-line, or couplet, units overlaid in the last one: *c d c d c d*.) Variations of the Italian form are the most common kind of sonnets in all languages.

The rhyme scheme is important because there is usually some correspondence between the units indicated by rhymes and the rhetorical content or thought development. The quatrains within the octave and the octave itself tend to be closed, to come to a complete stop. A **volta,** or turn, sets the sestet off in a new direction. But sonnets are rarely as simple as our explanation might suggest. One pattern overlays another. For instance, in the middle of the *a b b a a b b a* sequence of the octave is a quatrain (*b a a b*) within the quatrains. The octave, with its repeated rhymes and strict discipline, tends to be more orderly and rational, defining a problem or describing an experience, something to be reacted to in the sestet. The sestet, accordingly, tends to be more varied in structure and more emotional, and a great many opportunities for interplay of form and meaning are offered by those flexible tercets.

In the sixteenth century Sir Thomas Wyatt and the Earl of Surrey imported the sonnet into England, using the pentameter line which was emerging as the norm in our language. Already the rhymed couplet was a popular form (as we have seen in the sample of Chaucer in Chapter 5). Wyatt and Surrey began using the familiar rhymed couplet as a conclusion—something that almost never happened in sonnets written in Italy, France, or Spain. This poem of Wyatt's follows a generally Italian form, but notice the thumping couplet at the end, a very English twist:

> Whoso list to hunt, I know where is an hind,
>   But as for me, *helas!* I may no more.
>   The vain travail hath wearied me so sore,
> I am of them that furthest come behind.
> Yet may I, by no means, my wearied mind
>   Draw from the deer; but as she fleeth afore
>   Fainting I follow. I leave off therefore,
> Since in a net I seek to hold the wind.
> Who list her hunt, I put him out of doubt,
>   As well as I may spend his time in vain;
>   And graven with diamonds in letters plain
> There is written, her fair neck round about,
>   *"Noli me tangere,* for Caesar's I am,
>   And wild for to hold, though I seem tame."

The inscription that he imagines the lady (Anne Boleyn) wearing around her neck means "Nobody touch me!" Wyatt was disappointed at losing his mistress to Henry VIII. Indentations of lines are completely arbitrary, but these emphasize the structure of the two closed quatrains and the shape of the tercets. Notice the quatrain-couplet structure overlaid: *c d d c e e.* You can see the traditional *volta* at the beginning of the ninth line, indicated by the echo of the first line.

The next shift that was to appear in the emerging English form was to alternate rhymes in the quatrains: from *a b b a* to *a b a b.* You can see the form in transition in Sidney's "Loving in truth, and fain in verse my love to show," quoted in Chapter 1. Notice that the poem is in hexameter rather than pentameter. English poets tried various line lengths—and, indeed, various lengths of the sonnet. One of Shakespeare's sonnets was in tetrameter; another has only twelve lines. Spenser wrote some blank-verse sonnets (that is, in unrhymed iambic pentameter). Thomas Lodge has one consisting of four tetrameter quatrains and a pentameter couplet—eighteen lines. Giles Fletcher has an eighteen-line sonnet in pentameter. The word *sonnet* (which means "little song" or "little sound") was also used for short songlike poems in any form. (You can find examples in the work of Sir John Suckling.) These were clearly outside the sonnet tradition. But George Meredith's sequence of sixteen-line poems called *Modern Love* (in the nineteenth century) can best be understood as part of the sonnet tradition. (His poems consisted of four quatrains rhyming *a b b a c d d c e f f e g h h g.)*

What puts a poem inside or outside the sonnet tradition? One key characteristic is the aesthetic effect of one pattern superimposed on another, layer on layer—a tension between forms reflecting tensions in thought or feeling. What finally came to be accepted as the English sonnet (sometimes called Shakespearean sonnet, after its most prominent practitioner) rhymes *a b a b c d c d e f e f g g.* The two quatrains of the octave have different rhyme pairs, and there is a quatrain in the sestet built on the same pattern. The Italian sonnet used only four or five different rhyme sounds, making it necessary to find several words for each. The English pattern increases the number to seven, making it much easier to find rhymes. Most commentators say the English sonnet does away with the octave-sestet division, replacing it with a structure in which three independent quatrains form the body of the poem and the couplet is the response. But, in fact, this rarely happens. For example, here is Shakespeare's Sonnet 138:

> When my love swears that she is made of truth,
> I do believe her though I know she lies,
> That she might think me some untutored youth,
> Unlearnèd in the world's false subtleties.
> Thus vainly thinking that she thinks me young,
> Although she knows my days are past the best,
> Simply I credit her false-speaking tongue:
> On both sides thus is simple truth suppressed.

> But wherefore says she not she is unjust?
> And wherefore say not I that I am old?
> O love's best habit is in seeming trust,
> And age in love loves not to have years told.
>> Therefore I lie with her, and she with me,
>> And in our faults by lies we flattered be.

The eighth line clearly summarizes the problem. The ninth, with a *volta*, begins the response. Meanwhile the sestet is itself a kind of review of the whole sonnet. Its first two lines are questions responding to each of the two quatrains in turn. The *O* then starts an answer to the questions, and the couplet's two lines summarize in turn the octave and the sestet. Layer on layer, indeed, and yet the sonnet reads smoothly and dramatically, its intricate structure obscured by emotional intensity. If you look through a collection of sonnets you will see many ninth lines beginning with an *Ah* or *Oh* to mark the *volta*, introducing an emotional response to the problem in the octave. Yet there is almost always an interplay of other structures complicating this simple division.

I say all this so that you won't be too dogmatic about what is or isn't a sonnet. They are not mathematical exercises but poems reaching for a certain (or, rather, uncertain) something just beyond grasp. I believe that "something" has to do with the relation of form and content. Any good poet who accepts the challenge of the sonnet (and most have done so at least a few times in their careers) is intrigued by the question of how the thought development relates to the poem's form. Milton popularized crashing through the barrier between the octave and sestet. A sonnet such as his "Avenge, O Lord, thy slaughtered saints, whose bones" is a stem-winder, rolling out its full length with hardly a pause or redirection of the central idea. Such an innovation has force precisely because of the strength of the tradition. The reader's expectation (consciously or unconsciously) is for a *volta* that doesn't occur, or that occurs in an unexpected place.

The themes of sonnets have varied widely, too. Their original impetus was devotion to God. That was adapted to devotion to a goddesslike mistress in the tradition of courtly love. That, in turn, led to anti-courtly love sonnets such as the one above by Shakespeare (or his "My mistress' eyes are nothing like the sun"). Some of Milton's sonnets are political tracts. Sonnets have been used for satire, narrative, indeed for almost any subject imaginable. Here is a philosophical and satirical example by E. E. Cummings:

> pity this busy monster,manunkind,
>
> not, Progress is a comfortable disease:
> your victim (death and life safely beyond)
>
> plays with the bigness of his littleness
> —electrons deify one razorblade
> into a mountainrange;lenses extend
>
> unwish through curving wherewhen till unwish
> returns on its unself.
>   A world of made
> is not a world of born—pity poor flesh
>
> and trees,poor stars and stones,but never this
> fine specimen of hypermagical
>
> ultraomnipotence. We doctors know
>
> a hopeless case if—listen:there's a hell
> of a good universe next door;let's go

In spite of its self-conscious unconventionality of language and punctuation, it is a relatively conventional sonnet. You should be able to scan the pentameter without much difficulty. Notice the grouping of lines. The eighth is one line, though broken. The groups are of one, two, three, then three, two, and one lines, followed by a couplet, or group of two. The broken line occurs right in the middle of the poem, dividing it into equal parts.

Now look at the rhymes. All except two are off-rhymes. One sequence, the *a* rhymes, includes *manunkind, beyond, extend.* The *b* sequence includes *disease, littleness, unwish, flesh,* and *this*—words that have in common only their final sibilants. The *c*'s are the first true rhyme pair: *razorblade* and *made.* The *d*'s are *hypermagical* and *hell.* The *e*'s conclude the poem with the resonance of another pair of true rhymes, *know* and *go.* Thus the rhyme scheme is *a b a b c a b c b b d e d e.* What do you make of this? Notice that the poem begins and ends with quatrains: *a b a b* and *d e d e.* In the middle are two tercets, *c a b* and *c b b.* The quatrains are like those of English sonnets, the tercets like those of an Italian sestet. He has broken the octave in two and put the sestet in the middle. Notice how the broken eighth line leads into the *volta,* which is emphasized by the first of the two true rhyme pairs.

Many basic principles of form are illustrated by this poem. Tension makes poetry come alive, the pull of one element against another. There is a tension between the rather modern, slangy, technical vocabulary of the poem and its ancient form. Another is between the visual structure (represented by the one-two-three, etc., line groupings) and the sound structure implied by the rhyme scheme. Another is between the English and Italian forms of the sonnet. (The pair of lines at the end looks like an English rhymed couplet, but it doesn't rhyme.) Perhaps the deepest tension is that between the form of the poem and what it is saying. Its message is a protest against the "world of made," of artificiality, progress, science, and an affirmation of the "world of born," of naturalness, life. He says that "manunkind" enjoys (or is comfortable with) the disease of progress which is destroying the species. The case is hopeless. One might expect such a poem to be in free verse, kicking the traces of artifice and convention, wallowing in "natural" expression. But it outartifices the traditional artifice of the sonnet. The language is deliberately experimental and modern: "unwish through curving wherewhen till unwish / returns on its unself," language grappling imaginatively with the paradoxes of the Einsteinian universe, stretched in either direction to nothingness by electron microscopes and radiotelescopes, collapsing like the universe itself into the emptiness of matter and motion. Cummings was not a polemicist, but a poet. Were he writing a political pamphlet or philosophical tract he might eliminate or avoid the paradoxes in his protest. But as a poet he recognized the central place of paradox in grasping truth. So we have an ultramodernist, progressive poem denouncing modernism and progress, a glorification of nature that joyfully and ingeniously embodies extreme artifice. Notice that repeated *ih* sound in the opening phrase "Pity this busy . . ."; the nasals linking the surprising, dropped "not" to the phrase above; the way the repeated *en* sound in *lenses extend* stretches the phrase, pushing it into the vacant universe with an enjambment, yet tying it to the nasals in the next line and a half; the open, low vowels bringing the poem to its solidly rhymed, resonant conclusion:

> We doctors know
>
> a hopeless case if—listen:there's a hell
> of a good universe next door;let's go

And notice the ambiguity: that the universe next door seems for the instant of the line break to be a hell.

Each new twist a poet gives to the old form helps us to get another glimpse of that indefinable essence at the core. Read Shelley's "Ode to the West Wind," the first section of which was given in the last chapter. What does that poem gain by the allusion implicit in its form to a sonnet sequence (and to *terza rima*)? The form is a kind of comment on the tradition. It makes us cock our heads at a slightly different angle for another view of tradition.

Is this poem a sonnet?

For Once, Then, Something

Others taunt me with having knelt at well-curbs
Always wrong to the light, so never seeing
Deeper down in the well than where the water
Gives me back in a shining surface picture
Me myself in the summer heaven, godlike,
Looking out of a wreath of fern and cloud puffs.
Once, when trying with chin against a well-curb,
I discerned, as I thought, beyond the picture,
Through the picture, a something white, uncertain,
Something more of the depths—and then I lost it.
Water came to rebuke the too clear water.
One drop fell from a fern, and lo, a ripple
Shook whatever it was lay there at bottom,
Blurred it, blotted it out. What was that whiteness?
Truth? A pebble of quartz? For once, then, something.

My guess is that its author, Robert Frost, was playing with the conventions of the sonnet. There are fifteen lines, unrhymed. They have a curious metrical structure. Each begins with two trochees, then takes a little skip and continues with three iambs, but ends with a hypermetrical syllable, so it ends with a falling rhythm as it began. Alternatively, one might call these trochaic lines, with a dactyl (/ ˘ ˘) as the second foot:

> OTH ers \ TAUNT me with \ HAV ing \ KNELT at \
> WELL-curbs \

What you call it doesn't matter, but the strict consistency is intriguing. And it doesn't sound very sonnetlike.

But that italicized *Once* looks like a *volta,* starting the seventh line. That makes a sestet at the beginning—and in this case the sestet defines the problem: when we try to see into the depths we usually only see a reflection of ourselves, and are likely to mistake our image for a god. There are two tercets, the first describing the experience of looking into the well, the second describing the reflected image. Then we have an octave describing the exception, the one instance in which the poet got a glimpse of the depths. It is in two closed quatrains. The poem seems complete in fourteen lines, but, then, the fifteenth, the extra, comes as a kind of response to the whole poem. The word "Truth?" tells us what the poem has really been about.

I don't know whether Frost thought of the poem as a sonnet or not, but another of his poems seems much more definitely to be a fifteen-line sonnet. In his collected works it occurs between two more conventional sonnets, "Meeting and Passing and "The Oven Bird":

Hyla Brook

By June our brook's run out of song and speed.
Sought for much after that, it will be found
Either to have gone groping underground
(And taken with it all the Hyla breed
That shouted in the mist a month ago,
Like ghost of sleigh bells in a ghost of snow)—
Or flourished and come up in jewelweed,
Weak foliage that is blown upon and bent,

Even against the way its waters went.
Its bed is left a faded paper sheet
Of dead leaves stuck together by the heat—
A brook to none but who remember long.
This as it will be seen is other far
Than with brooks taken otherwhere in song.
We love the things we love for what they are.

The first eleven lines are devoted to a description of the pathetic brook (named for hyla, or tree frogs), which peters out and dries up in the summer. Their rhyme scheme suggests a kind of condensed sonnet: *a b b a c c a d d e e*. But then there is a quatrain, *f g f g*—and there is the real meat of the poem. Line 12 suggests that he is one who "remembers long," who cares. The next two lines contrast this poem with others about brooks (for example, Hopkins's "Inversnaid," which celebrates the stream's wet wildness). Stop. The poem comes to a halt after fourteen lines.

But, then, an afterthought. "Oh, I forgot to tell you—I love that shriveled-up little brook. My whole point is that we do not love fanciful ideals but real things, real people, with all their imperfections, the weaknesses which define them and make them what they are. We love them for *being* what they are." That single line speaks volumes. I say it to myself like a rosary, to remind me to have patience, to remember why I love.

This poem so craftily weaves in and out of sonnet patterns I think that "For Once, Then, Something" was a more radical experiment along the same lines. It is stretching the point, but I like to think of it as a sonnet about sonnets, about that search for inner essence which is so frustrated by surface forms.

Release your own imagination to that mystery.

11

Loose Ends

Blank Verse

Though both Classical Greek and Latin and Old English poetry were mostly unrhymed, poetry in English from the fourteenth until the sixteenth century was mostly rhymed. The emergence in the mid-sixteenth century of blank verse proved to be a liberating innovation. It has become almost the norm for longer poetic works, a durable medium for poetic drama, narrative, and many philosophical and didactic poems, and it is even used in short lyrics. On the other hand, free verse appeared occasionally in English from the Middle Ages on, but it became common only in the twentieth century and has been used primarily for short, intense, subjective lyrical poems.

Blank verse and **free verse** should not be confused. Blank verse has lines of consistent length and meter. Usually it is iambic pentameter, but some poets write blank tetrameter or hexameter, and combinations such as blank anapestic tetrameter or blank trochaic hexameter are possible variations. The term *blank* refers to lack of end-rhyme (though some end-rhyme and internal rhyme may occasionally occur in an unpatterned way). It is the basic underlying structure of general consistency of line length which makes blank verse work.

The term *free* in free verse (to be considered in the next chapter) refers to variations in line length. Free verse is often rhymed, and it can usually be scanned in normal metrical feet, but the line lengths have no consistent pattern. (Wordsworth's "Ode: Intimations of Immortality . . .," with its free-flowing strophes, could be called free verse, though I have never seen it so referred to.) Blank verse and free verse are responses to almost opposite needs of poets. Blank verse provides a way of maintaining poetic texture while the poet deals with necessary but relatively prosaic material—exposition, argument, dialogue, realistic representation, eloquent or rhetorical flights. The implication of free verse (since the time of the ancient Greeks) has always been that the speaker was "carried away," so inspired or seized by such overwhelming emotion that the bondage of consistent line length had to be thrown off. Meter means measure; specifically, measure of line length. When a poet abandons measure the conditions are, by implication, extraordinary. The poem makes the audience ask, What are these powerful forces at work that have broken down the basic premises of poetic form? When there is no poetic stance of being carried away, free verse tends to disintegrate into merely broken prose.

Blank verse was invented to provide an alternative to the incessant jingling of rhyme that characterized English poetry for two centuries. The other alternative was the continuing alliterative, accentual verse tradition, using essentially the meter of *Beowulf.* But heavy alliteration and stresses have their own kind of jingle; the sound devices attract so much attention to themselves that they distract from meaning. Such verse sounded something like this, the opening lines (in a modernized version) of *Sir Gawain and the Green Knight:*

> When the siege and assault   ceased at Troy, and the city
> Was broken, and burned   all to brands and to ashes,
> The warrior who wove there   the web of his treachery
> Tried was for treason,   the truest on earth.

I have discussed how Chaucer and his contemporaries freed up this congested form by developing what came to be known as accentual syllabic verse, using lines of consistent metrical length and end-rhyme. But perhaps because stresses were shifting bewilderingly in the process of melding various dialects into modern English, or perhaps because poets were unable to hear the music of Chaucerian meter, much English poetry of the fourteenth and fifteenth centuries was metrically ragged and lacked the cohesive structure of the alliterative tradition. Poets leaned heavily on rhyme to maintain a sense of poetry.

Here is a bit of a mid-sixteenth century poem, John Skelton's endless "Philip Sparrow":

When I remember again
How my Philip was slain,
Never half the pain
Was between you twain,
Pyramus and Thisbe,
As befell then to me:
The teares down hailed,
But nothing it availed
To call Philip again,
Whom Gib, our cat, hath slain.

One can see why an alternative was needed. The meter is shaky, and the rhymes seem almost desperate efforts to prop it up. Such poetry is called "Skeltonic," after the poet—and is sometimes imitated for humorous effect. But it is obviously not a very good medium for serious poetry, and when the matter requires longer lines, the meter disintegrates even more rapidly, as illustrated by these lines, also by Skelton:

O radiant luminary of light interminable,
    Celestial Father, potential God of might,
Of heaven and earth O Lord incomparable,
    Of all perfections the essential most perfite!

Much of the verse of these centuries was similarly clumsy and stumbling, held together by rhyme. Some was free verse by default: meter was simply abandoned. Other poems were written in some visual shape, such as Stephen Hawes's "A Pair of Wings." Its lines get longer and longer, then correspondingly shorter and shorter, to make the shape of wings on the page. Rhymes hold it together. Here is the beginning:

```
See
Me          (kind
Be
Againe
My paine        (in minde
Retaine
My sweete bloode
On the Roode        (my brother
Dide thee good
My face right redde
Mine armes spredde        (think none other
```

It is Jesus speaking; *Roode* (or *rood*) means "cross."

Meanwhile the spirit of the Renaissance was infusing English culture with the spirit of the Classics, and critics began complaining about "rude beggarly rhyming." We have already met, in earlier chapters, Wyatt and Surrey, two courtier poets of the mid-sixteenth century who did much to transform English poetry into the forms which have served till modern times. Wyatt introduced and Surrey refined the sonnet. But the Earl of Surrey also, almost single-handedly, invented English blank verse. Vergil's *Aeneid* was written in Latin unrhymed hexameter. Gavin Douglas, a Scots poet, had translated it into clumsy English rhymed couplets. Surrey adapted Douglas's work into unrhymed pentameter lines. Here is a sample:

> Lo, foremost of a rout that followed him,
> Kindled Laocoon hasted from the tower,
> Crying far off, O wretched citizens,
> What so great kind of frenzy fretteth you?
> Deem ye the Greeks, our enemies, to be gone?
> Or any Greekish gifts can you suppose
> Devoid of guile? Is so Ulysses known?
> Either the Greeks are in this timber hid
> Or this an engine is to annoy our walls,
> To view our towers and overwhelm our town.
> Here lurks some craft. Good Trojans, give no trust
> Unto this horse, for, whatsoever it be,
> I dread the Greeks—yea, when they offer gifts!

If this works for you, your attention stays on the action. You are following the story (of the Trojan horse), yet sensing the resonance and dignity and order of poetry.

For one thing, you should hear the meter ticktocking steadily but unobtrusively in the background. Scan it: the pentameter is quite regular, with normal variations. Of these thirteen lines, all but two are closed, but, overall, Surrey used enjambment about one-fourth of the time. With so much regularity of meter and closure of lines, there is a danger of monotony, which Surrey offset by varying the placement of caesuras. A couple of instances of initial alliteration stand out ("frenzy fretteth" and "Greekish gifts"), but generally his sound echoes are more subtle, though always rich. Listen to the *r, t, g, s,* and *k* sounds in this line: "H*e*re *l*urks *s*ome *c*raft. *G*ood *T*rojans, *g*ive no *tr*ust."

When writing blank verse you want to retain the feeling of poetry, yet avoid any excess which would draw too much attention to the language itself, away from its meaning. Merely breaking lines of prose into lines that look like poetry is obviously not sufficient to provide that feeling. When one reads such lines they still sound like prose. You have probably struggled with the problems that concerned Surrey. How do you know that a piece of your writing is poetry—that it is not just broken prose? If you were carried away, and the feeling was very passionate, or you had some startling images and figures of speech, or you were rhapsodizing about some very moving or inspiring experience, such questions might not have troubled your mind. But what about the rest of the time, when you were not especially inspired or moved or imaginative, but nonetheless had a job you wanted to do in poetry, not in prose? Many fall back on rhyme, especially if they are shaky in regard to meter. The first poem I remember writing, to my mother, when I was eight or nine, had a wobbly meter, just like English poetry of the fourteenth to mid-sixteenth century, but it was in rhymed couplets. I guess I composed the lines by thinking first of the rhymes, then finding sentences to put them in, letting the rhyme wag the rhythm. Most of my poetry is still rhymed (and metrical—smoother now, I hope). I still feel a little naked when the ends of my lines are hanging blankly loose.

But rhyme has its problems, especially in longer poems. The book-length philosophical and narrative poems of Chaucer, for instance, were all in couplets or elaborately rhymed stanzas, and, in spite of their grace

and pungency, they were obviously padded to fill out formal require-
ments, often with little words such as *ywis* (meaning "truly"), which gave
his poetry a colloquial flavor but diluted it in the process. To get the
right words into rhyme positions, poets have often wrenched the syntax,
twisted, inverted, settled for inexact words, filled in with syllables
unnecessary for meaning. And even when rhymed poetry is working well
and smoothly, the music may drown out the story (as in opera, in con-
trast to poetic drama). Surrey's innovation brought us a more limber
poetic mode, more easily adapted to natural-sounding speech, for telling
stories, presenting ideas, and, especially, creating powerful and believ-
able drama.

The possibilities of blank verse for the stage were quickly seen. A cou-
ple of blank-verse plays had already been produced when Christopher
Marlowe took up the form and forged his lines of thunder. His Tam-
burlaine (like many characters in his plays) specialized in ranting:

> Now clear the triple region of the air,
> And let the majesty of Heaven behold
> Their scourge and terror tread on emperors,
> And dim the brightness of their neighbor lamps!
> Disdain to borrow light of Cynthia!
> For I, the chiefest lamp of all the earth,
> First rising in the East with mild aspect,
> But fixèd now in the meridian line,
> Will send up fire to your turning spheres,
> And cause the sun to borrow light of you.

Cynthia is the moon goddess. Notice that every line is a closed unit—
Marlowe almost never used enjambment. Each line is to be belted out
with a new breath, as though the line were a single gigantic metrical foot
of ten syllables. There are few medial pauses. Sustaining such mouthfuls
requires sustaining relentless passion (the problem in free verse).
Marlowe's characters seem always to be living at emotional extremes.
T. S. Eliot commented that Marlowe's verse was "intractably poetic,"
and the job of later playwrights was to develop a blank-verse medium
that could "carry the burdens and exhibit the subtleties of prose."

Shakespeare (and others) taught us that blank verse need not be so
monotonous, that it could bear any burden a writer wants to put on it—

from low comedy to tender lovemaking to probing meditation to wily villainy, as when Iago begins planting the seed of jealousy of Cassio in Othello's head:

Iago:	Did Michael Cassio, when you woo'd my lady, Know of your love?
Othello:	He did, from first to last: why dost thou ask?
Iago:	But for a satisfaction of my thought. No further harm.
Othello:	Why of thy thought, Iago?
Iago:	I did not think he had been acquainted with her.
Othello:	O, yes; and went between us very oft.
Iago:	Indeed!
Othello:	Indeed! ay, indeed:—discern'st thou aught in that? Is he not honest?
Iago:	Honest, my lord!
Othello:	Honest! ay, honest.
Iago:	My lord, for aught I know.
Othello:	What dost thou think?
Iago:	Think, my lord!
Othello:	Think, my lord! By heaven, he echoes me, As if there were some monster in his thought Too hideous to be shown.—Thou dost mean something . . . .

The continuation of Othello's speech is in blank verse much more regular than that in the passage quoted. Such poetry has the transparency of prose, yet the prevailing regularity of meter and line length sharpens tension as content pulls against the form. The music is more intricate than simple pentameter. "Know of your love?" stands as a two-foot line, echoed by Iago's next partial line, "No further harm." His first "Indeed!" stands as a line. The exchange turning on the word "honest" stretches to six feet. Iago then has a three-foot line, "My lord, for aught I know." Then an exchange turning on the word "think" parallels the one on "honest," again stretching to six feet. (Two of these repetitions of "think" stand as monosyllabic feet.) Othello then has a three-foot line (paralleling Iago's), and the verse returns to normal pentameter. The repetitions of "indeed," then of "honest," then of "think" create a rat-a-tat pattern of dramatic intensity overlaid upon the steady iambic pentameter flow.

Thus, blank verse is a neutral, strong basic structure which can be varied with free-verse effects. It provides a texture, like the grain of the canvas in a painting, conveying depth and order regardless of surface variations. If you think that such a neutral texture makes no difference, look what happens when the passage is rewritten in modern prose, without meter:

Iago:	Did Michael Cassio know about your love of Desdemona during the time of your courtship?
Othello:	Yes, the whole time. Why?
Iago:	I just wondered. Think nothing of it.
Othello:	Why were you wondering, Iago?
Iago:	I didn't think he knew her, that's all.
Othello:	Oh, he knew her very well. He used to carry messages back and forth between us.
Iago:	Really?
Othello:	Really! Yes, really! Do you make something of that? He's honest, isn't he?
Iago:	Honest, my lord?
Othello:	Honest! Yes, isn't he honest?
Iago:	My lord, so far as I know he is.
Othello:	But what are you thinking?
Iago:	Thinking, my lord?
Othello:	Thinking, my lord! My God, he's repeating my words as though he had some monster in his mind so terrible he dare not show me.—You are implying something . . .

Do you hear the flatness? Do you now understand the answer to the question frequently asked of poets, Why not just write prose? Do you sense what we are missing in the modern theater, in which verse is practically unknown?

I have deliberately chosen passages of blank verse in which there are few figures of speech, few images, few of the more obvious devices of poetic language, so you could see why the meter itself makes such a difference. A five-foot line is long enough not to be choppy, not to trot (as tetrameter sometimes does), yet (unlike longer lines) it is short enough to be said in one breath.

Blank verse is the most malleable of forms in English verse, like basic black, salt in cooking, or, for that matter, the diatonic scale in music. Study the following adaptation of the form to comedy. Doto, the maid in Christopher Fry's modern play, *A Phoenix Too Frequent,* has decided to join her mistress in her master's tomb, where the two of them intend to die of grief and starvation. She says:

> It seemed quite lively then. And now I know
> It's what you say; life is more big than a bed
> And full of miracles and mysteries like
> One man made for one woman, etcetera, etcetera.
> Lovely. I feel sung, madam, by a baritone
> In mixed company with everyone pleased.
> And so I had to come with you here, madam,
> For the last sad chorus of me. It's all
> Fresh to me. Death's a new interest in life,
> If it doesn't disturb you, madam, to have me crying.
> It's because of us not having breakfast again.
> And the master, of course. And the beautiful world.
> And you crying too, madam. Oh—Oh!

Can you scan it? There are some tricky spots. The two *etcetera*'s have to be read as two variant feet, and those wails at the end are monosyllabic feet. You should be able to puzzle out the rest.

If blank verse can serve a comic turn, with bumps and stops and wild disconnectedness of thought, it is also versatile enough to be used for magnificent passages of great eloquence. When the tone is stately, the poet is more apt to use the full, closed, individually shaped line (such as Marlowe used). Here is the last (eighth) stanza of Wallace Stevens's "Sunday Morning":

> She hears, upon that water without sound,
> A voice that cries, "The tomb in Palestine
> Is not the porch of spirits lingering.
> It is the grave of Jesus, where he lay."
> We live in an old chaos of the sun,
> Or old dependency of day and night,
> Or island solitude, unsponsored, free,
> Of that wide water, inescapable.
> Deer walk upon our mountains, and the quail
> Whistle about us their spontaneous cries;
> Sweet berries ripen in the wilderness;
> And, in the isolation of the sky,
> At evening, casual flocks of pigeons make
> Ambiguous undulations as they sink,
> Downward to darkness, on extended wings.

That should be easier to scan than was Doto's speech. Stevens rolls out the full measure in a fairly regular meter in order to draw out the resonance of the line. It is difficult to sustain a passage in this manner without the verse sounding rhetorical or preachy.

To get a sense of the great variety of effects possible in blank verse, study passages of Milton's *Paradise Lost,* Browning's "Andrea del Sarto" or "Fra Lippo Lippi," Tennyson's "Ulysses," Yeats's "The Second Coming," Frost's "Birches" or "Mending Wall," or simply read a few of the plays of Shakespeare, almost any of which, if mastered, can provide you with a range of techniques for expressing just about anything in blank verse.

As I have pointed out, the devices of free verse may be used in a context of blank verse. A poet may use a partial line to indicate some extreme of emotion or of dramatic necessity. For example, when Shakespeare's King Lear has been subjected to unbearable indignities by his daughters, he begins protesting in rhetorical, blank verse, of shaped, closed lines. Then words fail him, and he breaks down near to sobbing—as indicated by a broken line:

> You see me here, you gods, a poor old man,
> As full of grief as age; wretched in both!

If it be you that stir these daughters' hearts
Against their father, fool me not so much
To bear it tamely; touch me with noble anger,
And let not women's weapons, water-drops,
Stain my man's cheeks!—No, you unnatural hags,
I will have such revenges on you both
That all the world shall—I will do such things—
What they are, yet I know not; but they shall be
The terrors of the earth. You think I'll weep,
No, I'll not weep:—
I have full cause of weeping; but this heart
Shall break into a hundred thousand flaws,
Or e'er I'll weep.—O fool, I shall go mad.

It is as though the half-line of silence after, "No, I'll not weep:—" were to give the actor a moment to touch the razor edge of tears and then gather himself, only to break from contained tears into the alternative horror of madness.

If you are thinking of trying your hand at blank verse, drama or narrative is a good place to start. To describe action or make credible speech you have to deal with a lot of neutral material, content that doesn't lend itself to a rich texture of images, flamboyant diction, or strident rhythmic effects. T. S. Eliot once used the term *transparency* for a kind of excellence which does not attract attention to itself. In a narrative such as Robert Frost's "Home Burial" we understand the story through the blank-verse medium as through a clean pane of glass. We enter the experience directly. The language is unadorned. There are almost no figures of speech. The meter is solid, strong, simple and subtle as bone structure. You have to peel back the words to see it.

The story—told in a mere 116 lines—is of a rural couple who have lost their first child. The husband has buried the child in the family plot, which can be seen from a window of the stair landing of their house. The poem is made up almost entirely of dialogue between the husband and wife on that stairway, dramatically moving up and down it and changing positions. It begins in tension, then snaps, a chasm opening between husband and wife. Here are the opening lines:

He saw her from the bottom of the stairs
Before she saw him. She was starting down,
Looking back over her shoulder at some fear.

The first line establishes the rhythm, varied only by a couple of pyrrhics (or theoretical iambs), but the second jerks us. You have to stress that first "she," putting a trochee in the unusual position of the second foot.

I will dwell on the line a moment to illustrate the multidimensional effects of meter (impossible in prose or free verse). The line seems to stand up off the page because of a kind of suspension of rhythm between the norm of alternating stress and the stresses demanded by sense. Meaning works a crosscurrent against the regular beat. I will repeat the line three ways below. The first illustrates the theoretical pattern. No one would read it that way because it doesn't make sense. The third shows phrasal grouping, the way the line would be read if it were prose. The middle way, indicating a proper scansion, is suspended between the other two:

be FORE \ she SAW \ him SHE \ was STAR \ ting DOWN \

be fore \ SHE saw \ HIM SHE \ was STAR \ ting DOWN \

be fore SHE \ saw HIM \ she was STAR \ ting DOWN \

As I have indicated, the third could be divided into feet: an anapest, iamb, anapest, and iamb. These would probably be the stresses of a conversational, rapid reading. But the pentameter context assures us that the poet would be unlikely to have intended a tetrameter line.

When we are thrown off the norm, as by the first, stressed "she," tension mounts. It continues in the third line:

LOOK ing \ BACK O \ ver her SHOUL \ der at \
SOME FEAR \

After such disturbance of the norm, a good poet senses the necessity of pulling back, reestablishing the basic meter (as announced in the first line). The fourth is the most regular so far, varied only by the hypermetrical syllable at the end:

she TOOK \ a DOUBT \ ful STEP \ and THEN \ un DID \ it

And the fifth is regular as well:

to RAISE \ her SELF \ and LOOK \ a GAIN. \ \ he SPOKE \

But the caesura late in the line and the sharp enjambment work to reintroduce tension.

For practice, scan the following lines yourself. Remember to dramatize as you go, putting the force into the words that the situation requires:

> He spoke
> Advancing toward her: "What is it you see
> From up there always?—for I want to know."
> She turned and sank upon her skirts at that,
> And her face changed from terrified to dull.
> He said to gain time: "What is it you see?"
> Mounting until she cowered under him.
> "I will find out now—you must tell me, dear."
> She, in her place, refused him any help,
> With the least stiffening of her neck and silence.
> She let him look, sure that he wouldn't see,
> Blind creature; and awhile he didn't see.
> But at last he murmured, "Oh," and again, "Oh."
>
> "What is it—what?" she said.
>   "Just that I see."
> "You don't," she challenged. "Tell me what it is."

When she sinks on her skirts, the beat becomes regular—and those last two lines of dialogue are surprisingly regular, in spite of their dramatic energy. Otherwise the poet does not let the lines rest for more than a couple of iambs in succession.

Look at what is happening. He mounts the stairs as though to capture her physically, though it is something subtler—her vision from the window—he is trying to grasp. She is cowering, stiff-necked, contemptuous but frightened. He is teetering between brute force and tenderness: "I will find out now—you must tell me, dear." It is difficult to know which syllables to stress in such a line. It has the tension of a pulled punch, with that weak, gentle, frustrated close.

We are nineteen lines into the poem, and the first crisis has subsided. We imagine him relaxing now, thinking he has solved the problem, easing into a conversational lyricism which calls for a much more even, regular pentameter than the preceding dramatic passage. Scan this one, too:

> "The wonder is I didn't see at once.
> I never noticed it from here before.
> I must be wonted to it—that's the reason.
> The little graveyard where my people are!
> So small the window frames the whole of it.
> Not so much larger than a bedroom, is it?
> There are three stones of slate and one of marble,
> Broad-shouldered little slabs there in the sunlight
> On the sidehill. We haven't to mind *those*.
> But I understand: it is not the stones,
> But the child's mound—"
>
>   "Don't, don't, don't, don't," she cried.

That last is a single line, though usually too long to be printed as one on the page, consisting of a pyrrhic, three spondees, and an iamb: a scream out against the husband's claim of understanding.

In the plainspoken, economical language of the poem, this speech of the husband is a little rhapsody, indulging (for the first time in the poem) in figures of speech, imagination, tenderness, sparking her violent protest. Notice also the closures. Six lines in succession consist of whole sentences, producing almost emotional stasis. You would not want to use such a monotonous, stable pattern unless you had good reason for it, as Frost has here.

She escapes him, dashes down the stairs, looks for her hat in a flurry, and the husband can hold her now only by promising not to pursue: "Listen to me. I won't come down the stairs." Her hostility is as ancient as our separate genders. He is, she claims, too crude and insensitive even to speak of his dead child, or of much else that requires delicacy of feeling. Stalemate:

"There's something I should like to ask you, dear."

"You don't know how to ask it."

"Help me, then."

Her fingers moved the latch for all reply.

Notice the steadiness of the meter in those lines, grim and careful in a still moment when any mistake might set off flame or flight.

She doesn't think any *man* can speak with caring of things that matter, and he feels unmanned by the requirement this puts upon their living together. The poem risks one formidable polysyllable when no other word will do to express the theme of the poem. The husband says:

"I do think, though, you overdo it a little.
What was it brought you up to think it the thing
To take your mother-loss of a first child
So inconsolably—in the face of love.
You'd think his memory might be satisfied—"

One is reminded of inconsolable Hamlet, of the bottomless pit of grief that put him out of touch with the world. But the very word is a challenge, which she takes as sarcasm, accusing him of "sneering," which, in turn, makes him explode in anger.

One can hear the tears and hysteria in her voice as she describes the gravedigging:

"If you had any feelings, you that dug
With your own hand—how could you?—his little grave;
I saw you from that very window there,
Making the gravel leap and leap in air,
Leap up, like that, like that, and land so lightly
And roll back down the mound beside the hole.
I thought, Who is that man? I didn't know you.
And I crept down the stairs and up the stairs
To look again, and still your spade kept lifting."

The alliteration intensifies the effect of the regular iambs in this passage. The lines leap; then, with dark low vowels, roll down the mound to the hole.

What should he have done? *Not* dig the grave? One can imagine as much reverence in his act of digging as in her squeamishness about it. She is especially upset by the words she heard rumbling in the kitchen after he had finished:

> "I can repeat the very words you were saying:
> 'Three foggy mornings and one rainy day
> Will rot the best birch fence a man can build.'
> Think of it, talk like that at such a time!
> What had how long it takes a birch to rot
> To do with what was in the darkened parlor?"

The answer, of course, unstated in the poem, is that those words are themselves a poetic mourning, a comment on transience and futility of human endeavor, a meditation on mutability. But she is deaf to his poetry—and feels tarnished by the merest contact with reality:

> "But the world's evil. I won't have grief so
> If I can change it. Oh, I won't, I won't!"

Notice how the staccato nervousness of her speech contrasts with the steady beat of the words she quotes from him. You can hear his masculine rumble right through her feminine shrillness.

There is no resolution. He thinks that since she spilled all that out of her system, the crisis is over. This *is* male insensitivity, male blindness to the needs and purposes of women. She still intends to leave, and he is suddenly, helplessly, almost comically, one might say almost femininely, reduced to a sudden concern with appearances, what folks will think:

> "Amy! There's someone coming down the road!"
> "*You*—oh, you think the talk is all. I must go—
> Somewhere out of this house. How can I make you—"
>
> "If—you—do!" She was opening the door wider.
> "Where do you mean to go? First tell me that.
> I'll follow and bring you back by force. I will—"

And that ends the poem. His resort to the threat of force confirms her judgment of him. His effort to hold merely estranges.

The meter of these last lines goes ragged as the feelings until we hear the steady clomp of his assertiveness. The third from the last line, " 'If—you—do!' She was opening the door wider," is almost unscannable. Each of the first three words seems to require a stress, then the line collapses with a string of unaccented syllables:

IF YOU \ DO she \ was O \ pen ing the \ DOOR WID \ er

The fourth foot could be called a tribrach, such as we saw Frost using in "Mowing," or one might imagine a slight stress on *ing,* making it an amphibrach; or one can pronounce the word *OPning,* making the fourth foot a pyrrhic; or one can sort out the jumble some other way. It hardly matters. The raggedness makes its poetic point—a pileup of intensity, then confused slackening, before the solid iambic determination of the last two lines.

None of these special effects could be achieved without that neutral, unobtrusive iambic pentameter base which pumps along like the systolic and diastolic pulsing of the heart, pumps along in our subconscious as we read, once we are given the signals, such as the first line of this poem and the frequent return to regularity. Some regard iambic meter as a yoke, but I hope you are discovering that the yoke is easy, that true freedom is within it, that one can hardly pull a weight such as "Home Burial" without it, and that intensity requires a container strong enough to press powerfully against.

12

Carried Away

Free Verse

When the discussion of Robert Frost's "Home Burial" (in Chapter 11) first appeared (in my column in *Writer's Digest*), a reader commented in a letter to me, "I can't believe Frost bothered with counting feet and syllables and all those technical things. He was a poet, not a mechanic. He listened to his heart, and the music poured forth." Well, it is amazing that it poured in such craftily varied regularity. My correspondent was unconsciously echoing the theme of Sir Philip Sidney's sonnet quoted in Chapter 1: "Look in thy heart and write." It was not original with Sidney. One of the most ancient postures of the artist has been that of one inspired, carried away, the Aeolian harp through which divine music flows.

This is the posture of the free-verse poet. I call it a "posture" because, frankly, I don't believe it is often, if ever, a genuine explanation for where poetry comes from. Sidney gave the game away by seeming to advocate spontaneous expression in an intricately crafted sonnet. Any intelligent reader could see that the poem was not a simple pouring forth of the heart's excess. Free verse is more deceptive. It *looks* as though the poet were actually carried away. It is the use of form to convey the illusion of spontaneity.

It is difficult to know how serious poets are when they claim inspiration. I call it the Mammy Yokum attitude, referring to the cartoon character in *Li'l Abner* who periodically spun in a trance and received messages from the Beyond. Regularly I hear from Mammy (and Pappy!) Yokums around the country who tell me they just write what "comes," and, indeed, the examples they send me seem not to have been subjected to much rational thought or to have much clear intent. But the occult infests poetry at more sophisticated levels, too. James Merrill has produced (in three books) a long poem which *Newsweek* compares to Dante's *Divine Comedy,* a poem "dictated" to Merrill and his friend David Jackson by a Ouija board. "I have taken this down by dictation," Merrill said in an interview. Rather than author, he is more like an editor, for "It seemed unethical to use it verbatim. Rather like plagiarism."

Many modern poets seem to be eager to disclaim responsibility for what they have written (and their poems often suggest they have good reason). An essay by poet Tess Gallagher (*Atlantic*, May 1980) is a rather typical expression of the quasi-religious attitude which has become so pervasive in modern poetry. She describes her creative process as one in which she is a passive "witness." The images just come. The poem takes on a life of its own and speaks with itself. What it means is something no one, not even the poet, can say definitively. She quotes the Mexican poet and critic Octavio Paz, who describes "the" poem as "the space that is energy itself, not a container but an engenderer, a catalytic arena open on all sides to the past, on all sides to the future." That sounds to me like mumbo jumbo, the sort of paradoxical language used to describe mystical experiences.

I don't deny that some poets have had mystical experiences and that such experiences have been the basis for good poems. Some of my own poetry (some rather good, some dreadful) has "just come" to me, and I recorded relatively spontaneous words and thought. But when poets and critics talk about "the" poem in this way, they imply a norm—one that would encompass all the poems of, say, Chaucer, Shakespeare, Pope, Browning, Frost, even of Edgar Guest. Such talk seems to me dangerous nonsense.

The implication is that one cannot learn to write poems. They happen. The emphasis is not upon craft but upon the nature of the poet, who is a chosen priest or priestess or medium or oracle transmitting a sacred text. Whether the resulting poetry is free or metrical is irrelevant, though most of it tends to be free (as metrical form implies too much control and forethought). In earlier times, poems were clearly products of craft. They told stories, dramatized, entertained, conveyed experiences, communicated ideas and values. They were assumed to be very much under the control of the poet (though, as a matter of convention, many poets ascribed their inspiration to the muse, or pretended, as Sidney did, to utter free-flowing sentiments of the heart). If a reader understood something the author had not intended, communication had broken down. Either the poet didn't write well or the reader didn't read well. But in today's cultural climate it is widely assumed about poetry and the other arts that anything goes, either in the making or in the interpretation.

Perhaps because of widespread disillusionment with conventional forms of religion, art has become a surrogate religion. People look to poetry for ultimate truths—not in the form of moral prescription or philosophical exposition, but in the form of mystic utterance, cryptic as an oracle, delivered by a special kind of person, one with a "gift" for receiving revealed truth. In such a climate, the emphasis is not upon what a poet *does* but what a poet *is*. If you want to write poetry, be inspired. No need to study, to count feet or syllables. That is the way to be a mechanic.

I cannot tell you how to be inspired, or to detect phony inspiration in yourself or others. But I can, I think, show you that free verse has techniques just like any other form of verse, that some techniques work better than others, and that posture, or the attitude assumed by the poet, is of prime importance in this kind of poetry.

First, as mentioned in the last chapter, you should recognize that freedom in free verse is basically one of *line length*. Flexibility of line length (or of measure) has always, since the ancient Greeks, been a signal to the audience that the poet (or speaker of the poem) was carried away. Variation in line length asks a kind of indulgence of the audience, saying, in effect, "Look, folks, I know I am violating your expectations and my own sense of form, but I can't help it right now. I just have to get this off my chest. Forget about formalities."

For example, study the mid-nineteenth century poem "Dover Beach" by Matthew Arnold, which begins with these lines:

> The sea is calm to-night.
> The tide is full, the moon lies fair
> Upon the straits;—on the French coast the light
> Gleams and is gone; the cliffs of England stand, . . .

The mood here is not of extreme emotion, but probing, thoughtful meditation, and the poet slowly builds up to a pentameter norm with a three-foot line, a four-foot line, then pentameter. If you read the rest of the poem you will find that he maintains that pentameter (rhymed in an arbitrary fashion) until the last two lines of the first strophe, when he drops back to tetrameter. In the remaining three strophes the lines are freely varied from three to five feet (a hinge line, "The Sea of Faith," has only two). The whole poem can be scanned as iambic, with the normal variations we have studied.

We associate free verse with the "modernist" movement in American and European poetry in the early decades of this century, but its patterns were already well established. In Chapter 3 we looked at Whitman's free verse, cadenced much like the King James Version of the Bible. (He was also strongly influenced by operatic arias.) Whitman's contemporary, Emily Dickinson, used basically a ballad (or hymn) stanza of alternating four- and three-foot lines, but her variations were so radical that sometimes the original form is hard to recognize. She starts this poem in pentameter, and then abandons that meter:

> After great pain, a formal feeling comes—
> The Nerves sit ceremonious, like Tombs—
> The stiff Heart questions was it He, that bore,
> And Yesterday, or Centuries before?
>
> The Feet, mechanical, go round—
> Of Ground, or Air, or Ought—
> A wooden way
> Regardless grown,
> A Quartz contentment, like a stone—
>
> This is the Hour of Lead—
> Remembered, if outlived,
> As Freezing persons, recollect the Snow—
> First—Chill—then Stupor—then the letting go—

This is the authoritative text published in 1955 by Harvard University Press, which restores the form Dickinson actually used. (Earlier versions in print are distorted by the tinkering of various editors.) Why did she make two lines of "A wooden way / Regardless grown."? Had she put all that on one line, the stanza would at least be a quatrain, rhyming *a a b b* like the others, though the number of feet per line would not be consistent. Presumably she was carried away. She broke the line for special emphasis, or clarity, or simply because she felt like it. Notice that the final couplet returns to the pentameter of the opening stanza.

Another nineteenth-century American poet, Ralph Waldo Emerson, occasionally used free-verse methods. In his "Hamatreya" there is a section called "Earth Song" in which the Earth is commenting on the vanity and transience of human ownership of Earth:

> "Mine and yours;
> Mine, not yours.
> Earth endures;
> Stars abide
> Shine down in the old sea;
> Old are the shores;
> But where are the old men?
> I who have seen much,
> Such have I never seen."

The "Earth Song" goes on in this manner for four strophes (of, respectively, nine, seven, nine, and seven lines)—then the poet responds in his own voice:

> When I heard the Earth-song
> I was no longer brave;
> My avarice cooled
> Like lust in the chill of the grave.

The free verse here suggests a supernatural, mystical experience. Similarly, the parablelike poems of Stephen Crane were like short broken paragraphs, drawing their authority for abandonment of meter from something like religious inspiration, suggestive of the Gnostic tradition:

In the desert
I saw a creature, naked, bestial,
Who, squatting upon the ground,
Held his heart in his hands,
And ate of it.
I said, "Is it good, friend?"
"It is bitter—bitter," he answered;
"But I like it
Because it is bitter,
And because it is my heart."

That little phrase "ate of it" has a biblical echo—and is a clue to the poet's intention. He is taking the stance of the prophet. He can't help it if his lines are flat, unmusical, prosaic. That's how they came to him. One reads such poetry purely for the content, for the "wisdom" or vision it contains, less than for the use of language as art. Such a poem would lose little in translation to another language. Only the line breaks make it poetic.

These are some of the precedents poets had in the early twentieth century when they felt stifled by their cultural climate, broke out in rebellion, kicking the traces, casting off traditional forms. One of the first things they chose to thumb their noses at was the expectation that lines of poetry would have a predictable number of feet per line or, indeed, any rationale at all for poetic form. Though most of their work was lyrical, here is a strophe from a narrative by Amy Lowell, "Patterns":

In a month he would have been my husband.
In a month, here, underneath this lime,
We would have broke the pattern;
He was for me, and I for him,
He as Colonel, I as Lady,
On this shady seat.
He had a whim
That sunlight carried blessing.
And I answered, "It shall be as you have said."
Now he is dead.

The rhythm does not vary much from an iambic norm; the rhymes are irregularly spaced but persistent. Most lines are closed, the line breaks being used almost as a kind of punctuation.

Free verse for the early modernist poets was not the exception but the rule. It was not a device to be used at special times of great intensity of feeling. It was the norm. They were carried away all the time. Blank verse, remember, came as a stabilizing force, a means for maintaining a sense of poetic texture, for providing unobtrusive richness. But free verse, especially when linked to the forces of self-conscious modernism and rebellion, is a disruptive force, seizing attention, implying by its very nature some uncontrollable emotion or mood or mystical force.

Why not be intense all the time? It might be argued that to qualify as poetry at all, language should be so intensely felt that any thought of formal regularity would be a violation of its raw power. Modernist poets (remember, this "modernism" is of the era of the Model T) tried to achieve a sensitive, original, momentary responsiveness to content, shaping their lines according to the feeling and intent of the poem, asserting individuality, strong will, and a mysterious, indefinable capacity that made poets different from other mortals.

Unrelieved intensity is a hard act to follow. At times this approach produced works of great beauty and power, as in T. S. Eliot's "The Hollow Men" (available in most anthologies of modern poetry; look it up and read the whole poem). This poem is grand and visionary in manner (much in the vein of Emerson's "Earth Song" from "Hamatreya"). The poet drapes himself in the robes of an oracle or prophet and utters wisdom mystically received. Hence we don't expect literal sense. In the first line "We are the hollow men." In the second, "We are the stuffed men." The contradiction is apparently deliberate: we are like dummies, empty of soul. In the next lines we learn our "headpiece" is "filled with straw." This seems to suggest scarecrows—but not a lonely scarecrow in a field. Apparently, we are a group of them, "Leaning together." As the strophe continues we find we are in a cellar with broken glass on the floor with rats crawling over it—a strange place for scarecrows. Obviously the poem is not intended to make literal sense. Oracles and prophets tend not to be very coherent. But the rhythms of the poem are authoritative, strong, and strange, sounding vaguely biblical, something like a chant or prayer. The enjambments are subtle and tense, as in:

> Remember us—if at all—not as lost
>   Violent souls, but only
>   As the hollow men . . .

In such poems the poet assumes the stance of an oracle, of an Aeolian harp (one played by the wind). or passive instrument of supernatural will. Free verse is appropriate, for the poet is (or pretends to be) out of control. Another stance which seems to evoke much free verse is that of the **bard**—a kind of "official" poet whose job requires him to celebrate institutions, heroes, victories, or other aspects of society (or sometimes, in its negative form, to lambaste society in vituperation or satire). Much of Whitman's work was bardic in this sense, and he has influenced many American poets from Edgar Lee Masters, Carl Sandburg, Robinson Jeffers, and Kenneth Fearing to Allen Ginsberg and other current poets. Such poetry has a suggestion of platform eloquence, of public speaking, as in the opening of Carl Sandburg's "Chicago":

> Hog Butcher for the World,
> Tool Maker, Stacker of Wheat,
> Player with Railroads and the Nation's Freight Handler
> Stormy, husky, brawling,
> City of the Big Shoulders:
> They tell me you are wicked and I believe them, for I have seen
>   your painted women under the gas lamps luring the farm
>   boys.
> And they tell me you are crooked and I answer: Yes, it is true I
>   have seen the gunman kill and go free to kill again.

The lines are closed, the rhythm pumping and strong, though irregular, and much use is made of rhetorical devices such as balance and parallelism. One does not experience the subtleties, ironies, tensions, and probing thought often associated with lyric poetry. Oracular and bardic poems are very public. The "I" is a kind of stage figure rather than the poet speaking in his own voice.

But free verse is also used for intensely personal poems, when the emotion that carries the poet away is not religious inspiration or platform eloquence, but rambling free association, sexual passion, rhapsodic joy, or some other overwhelming feeling. In Sylvia Plath's "Fever 103°"

it is delirium. Here is the conclusion of the poem:

> I am too pure for you or anyone.
> Your body
> Hurts me as the world hurts God. I am a lantern—
>
> My head a moon
> Of Japanese paper, my gold beaten skin
> Infinitely delicate and infinitely expensive.
>
> Does not my heat astound you! And my light!
> All by myself I am a huge camellia
> Glowing and coming and going, flush on flush.
>
> I think I am going up,
> I think I may rise—
> The beads of hot metal fly, and I love, I
>
> Am a pure acetylene
> Virgin
> Attended by roses,
>
> By kisses, by cherubim,
> By whatever these pink things mean!
> Not you, nor him
>
> Nor him, nor him
> (My selves dissolving, old whore petticoats)—
> To Paradise.

The triplets, usually closed but sometimes startlingly enjambed—as in the "I / Am" above—give a kind of formal consistency to the poem, but for the most part Plath depends on rich sound texture, occasional internal and end-rhymes and off-rhymes as formal devices. What makes the poem powerful—and this is true of much free verse—is spectacular imagery and racing thought patterns.

When the emotional level is less intense, and the language is less charged with imagination, free verse may, indeed, seem merely broken prose. What makes these lines poetry?

> To the sea they came—
> 2000 miles in an old bus
> fitted with brittle shelves and makeshift beds
> and cluttered with U.S. canned goods
>   —to the Sea!
> on which they paddle
> innertubes   —and the lowhovering Sun—
> from which the old woman hides her head
> under what looks like
> a straw wastebasket.
>   "Yep, they cured me alright,
> but see, it made my breasts grow like a woman's."
> And she: "Something hurts him in his chest,
> I think
>   maybe it's his heart,"—and her's
> I can see beating at the withered throat.

That is the first strophe of "Pure Products" by Denise Levertov. It is poetry only because she says it is, and the Bureau of Standards has no specifications which can prove her wrong. She is one of the abler poets writing this kind of generally low-key, flat, unrhythmic poetry in completely arbitrary or whimsical line lengths. In my view it would save space and not seriously alter the effectiveness or meaning of the poem to print it as a prose poem—a paragraph not using the line as a unit.

I have argued that accentual syllabic poetry, especially iambic pentameter, has an organic relationship to the inner nature of our language, but free-verse poets have claimed quite the opposite—that it distorts the language and a new measure must be found to break the iambic yoke. Here is William Carlos Williams, writing in the *Princeton Encyclopedia of Poetry and Poetics:*

> The crux of the question is measure. In free verse the measure has been loosened to give more play to vocabulary and syntax—hence, to the mind in its excursions. The bracket of the customary foot has been expanded so that more syllables, words, or phrases can be admitted into its confines. The new unit thus created may be called the "variable foot," a term and a concept already accepted widely as a means of bringing the warring elements of freedom and dis-

cipline together. It rejects the standard of the conventionally fixed foot and suggests that measure varies with the idiom by which it is employed and the tonality of the individual poem. Thus, as in speech, the prosodic pattern is evaluated by criteria of effectiveness and expressiveness rather than mechanical syllable counts. The verse of genuine poetry can never be "free," but free verse, interpreted in terms of the variable foot, removes many artificial obstacles between the poet and the fulfillment of the laws of his design.

The term "variable foot," which Williams invented, has not, in fact, gained wide acceptance, for there is no way to tell what it means. Does a line consist of a given number of variable feet? How can you tell? Is a whole line one foot, or an arbitrarily broken third of a line? I say "third" because Williams, apparently trying to illustrate variable feet, typically broke the lines of much of his later poetry into three parts:

```
Of asphodel, that greeny flower,
        like a buttercup
                upon its branching stem—
save that it's green and wooden—
        I come, my sweet,
                to sing to you.
We lived long together
        a life filled,
                if you will,
with flowers. So that
        I was cheered
                when I came first to know
that there were flowers also
        in hell.
                Today
I'm filled with the fading memory of those flowers
        that we both loved,
                even to this poor
colorless thing—
```

Is each of the three parts a foot? Many can be read with one stress, but others cannot be read that way. Maybe stress has nothing to do with it. Certainly phrasing has nothing to do with it—nor does idiom, natural-ness, expressiveness, effectiveness, or what you will. What do we make of a foot such as "with flowers. So that"?

So far as I can tell, if this is a way of bringing the warring elements of freedom and discipline together, it does so by defeating discipline entirely. I can't see that these lines gain anything whatsoever from being broken into three parts, or, indeed, from being written in lines of verse. As a prose poem, it would read like this:

> Of asphodel, that greeny flower, like a buttercup upon its branching stem—save that it's green and wooden—I come, my sweet, to sing to you. We lived long together a life filled, if you will, with flowers. So that I was cheered when I came first to know that there were flowers also in hell. Today I'm filled with the fading memory of those flowers that we both loved, even to this poor colorless thing.

It is disjointed prose, not very effective or expressive (or coherent), but is, in this form, at least free of pretense. I like it even better as iambic pentameter—blank verse—which we can get by reversing two words in the fourth line:

> Of asphodel, that greeny flower, like
> a buttercup upon its branching stem—
> save that it's green and wooden—I come, my sweet,
> to sing to you. We lived together long
> a life filled, if you will, with flowers. So
> that I was cheered when I came first to know
> that there were flowers also in hell. Today
> I'm filled with the fading memory of those
> flowers that we both loved, even to this
> poor colorless thing.

Williams wrote so naturally in the alternating stress normal to English poetry that he may not have realized it was the iambic texture which made his free verse musical. Much of his earlier poetry was in straightforward accentual syllabic meter, and the echoing fragments of traditional poetry stayed with him, for all his self-conscious modernism.

From these examples you may derive some principles for your own guidance in writing free verse. If you want long lines, as used by Whitman and those in his tradition, they probably should be closed, definite rhetorical units, sustained by a strong cadence and frequent parallelism. It is a form best adapted to the bardic stance, the public speech, the pronouncement, because its sonority and rhetorical quality make it seem stilted for other purposes.

You will find short lines generally more effective. These permit enjambment, which is the one device most commonly relied upon by free-verse poets for impact. Surprising enjambments are not surprising if used too often, so the technique is limited. Probably not only the lines but the poems themselves will be short (twenty lines or less). It is difficult to maintain the intensity of strong emotion and tension in longer poems. (Sylvia Plath's "Fever 103°" is an exception, as are several other of her poems; but, as free-verse poets go, she was remarkably metrical, used rhyme powerfully, and tended to use stanzalike strophes which give the appearance of symmetry and design to her free verse.)

If you do not have the support of measure, you will probably draw more heavily on other poetic elements to maintain the sense that your poem is indeed a poem, not just broken prose. These include strong imagery, strong rhythms, irregular but frequent rhymes and other kinds of sound echo. Incoherence amounts almost to a technique. A reader expects it of someone who is carried away. For this reason free-verse poets use startling juxtapositions, abrupt transitions, darting syntax, incomplete sentences, strange diction. In some ways free verse resembles the "stream of consciousness" technique in fiction, an effort to simulate the unfettered rambling of reverie or dream states. Time and logic are often distorted, as in dreams. The poem seems to ride the burning point of now, as though the poet had no past or future, only the hot moment of present consciousness. Often there is an affectation of derangement or of surrealism, characteristics imitative of dreams.

The stance or posture I have described is also a technique. You have to be subtle about it, not blatant as Shakespeare's John of Gaunt, who said, "Methinks I am a prophet new-inspired." But in some way you are inviting attention to the speaker in the poem as a special sort of person, be it prophet or oracle or madman or some other figure so caught up in the rush of inspiration as to cast off the bondage of meter. We have seen how flat free verse becomes when it lacks that posture.

But free verse may now be exhausted as a technique. Echoes of old music made the free verse of the early part of our century effective. Today the norm is mere randomness or arbitrariness of line length, without those echoes. Free verse has become no more than broken prose. It is no longer a rebellion. If a poet wants to be rebellious today, he or she will have to write in meter. There is no longer a norm of metrical verse to rebel against. The modernist movement began to dominate literary or intellectual poetry nearly a century ago. By now a generation of teachers has grown up accepting and passing on free verse as standard. Few people these days are taught to hear meter. Poets have a long, hard job ahead if they wish to restore music and measure to poetry.

The effect of saturation of a culture with free verse is ironic. When being carried away becomes the normal state, it is no longer poetic in its effect. There have been few efforts to use free verse for longer forms. Imagine a *Paradise Lost* or *Hamlet,* or even "Home Burial," in free verse! Such a major undertaking would quickly break down into prose.

These longer forms have almost disappeared from the poetic scene, and most poetry published now is in the form of short, intense, personal lyrics, the genre to which free verse is most suited. Another factor is that most poems are first published in magazines, where they are used as filler material in the spaces at the ends of prose pieces, so there is a premium on brief, sensational poems. All these tendencies combine to create an impression that poetry is ragged, nervous, broken, highly subjective self-expression such as few people care to read. The modernist movement started in the early years of this century as an effort to reach out to a new readership, to create a larger audience for poetry. For a time it succeeded in doing that, but as modernism creaks on through its second half-century, it is alienating readers and dulling the ears and sensitivities of those few it retains.

You may be the one to find a way to reach out anew to a popular audience with poetry that sings, and its singing may not be that of accentual or of accentual syllabic meter, but some new form yet to be invented. But I predict it will not be through further loosening of the discipline of measured verse.

13

Flesh on the Bones

Imagery and Symbolism

So far we have mainly discussed the form of poetry and have not said much about its content, which is a little like talking about a skeleton without its flesh. It makes sense to do so, however. There is not as much difference between the meat of a mouse and that of a monkey as there is between their bone structures. Poetry differs from prose primarily because of its form: its lines, stanzas, strophes, verse paragraphs, meter, and sound combinations, including rhyme.

But many readers (and poets) think of poetry as having a very special kind of content, unique to itself. Think about that for a moment before reading on. Are there some kinds of things said or communicated in poetry which are not communicated in prose? Can you tell by content (regardless of form) whether a piece of writing is poetry or prose? I'll test you on your answer below.

One answer you might give is that poetry *tends* to communicate through images and symbols rather than through statement. In this chapter I will discuss and illustrate the varieties of images and symbols, but they are by no means peculiar to poetry, nor does poetry always use them. Poetry such as that quoted from Pope's "An Essay on Criticism" in Chapter 5 is called "didactic" because it instructs. But it is also some-times called **poetry of statement** because its primary communication is through expository sentences; though it uses images and symbols abun-

dantly, these tend to decorate or illustrate the meaning. In other kinds of
poetry the images and symbols are more integral to what the poem says
or is about. Some (especially modern poets and critics) contend that
poetry should communicate entirely by images and symbols.

Before I define these terms, however, I would like to test your notions
of the appropriate content for poetry and prose. Below are six uniden-
tified passages of twentieth-century writing. To disguise their form, I
have arranged them all as poetry. Some are from novels, some are from
poems. Can you tell the difference?

1

At home, in my flannel gown, like a bear to its floe,
I clambered to bed; up the globe's impossible sides
I sailed all night—till at last, with my black beard,
My furs and my dogs, I stood at the northern pole.

2

The handle of the scimitar, bronze worked
To imitate wound cord, nearly fell from my hand,
So unexpectedly ponderous was the blade.
In this life woven of illusions and
Insubstantial impressions it is gratifying
To encounter heft, to touch the leaden center
Of things, the *is* at the center of *be,* the rock
In Plato's cave. I thought of an orange.

3

Now the fire had dwindled to powdery ash before
Uther Pendragon did unjoin himself,
Though now much against the will of the fair
Ygraine, but as after much killing even a king
Must rest, so in love, and he did stretch his limbs
And cool himself and clear his throat and then,
Thrusting his tongue into the cavern of
His cheek, he spake as follows.

4

And it seemed she was like the sea, nothing but dark
Waves rising and heaving, heaving with a great swell,
So that slowly her whole darkness was in motion,
And she was ocean rolling its dark, dumb mass.

5

I was alone, leaning on the tree, shivering. I listed to the wind.
Below the thick, gnarled roots of the oak there was no firm ground,
But a void, a bottomless abyss, and there were voices—sounds
Like the voices of leaves, I thought, or the babble of children, or
    gods.

6

He sits at the table, head down, the young clear neck exposed,
Watching the drugstore sign from the tail of his eye;
Tatoo, neon, until the eye blears, while his
Solicitous tall sister, simple in blue, bending
Behind him, cuts his hair with her cheap shears.

Scan them. All are pentameter except number 5, which is hexameter. All use anapests freely. You might find number 5 hardest to scan, for it is not accentual syllabic, but, rather, is accentual, with six beats to the line, yet often with as many as four unaccented syllables between stresses. That one was written as poetry—in John Gardner's modern epic, *Jason & Medeia*. So was the first—the beginning of Randall Jarrell's "90 North." The second was written as prose—in John Updike's *The Coup*, which I arbitrarily broke into lines approximating iambic pentameter (except for the last, which has only four feet). The third is also prose, from Thomas Berger's modern treatment of the Arthurian legends, *Arthur Rex*, but it lends itself surprisingly smoothly to pentameter breaks (except for, again, the last line, which has only three feet). The fourth is also prose, from D. H. Lawrence's *Lady Chatterley's Lover;* it breaks so naturally into iambic pentameter lines that one might almost think it was written with that in mind. The sixth is a stanza from a poem by Muriel Rukeyser, "Boy With His Hair Cut Short" (which I will discuss at length later). I opened books more or less at random to find these passages, and just started typing, breaking the prose into lines as I went. I hope the experiment demonstrates to you, as it does to me, that there need be no real difference in content between poetry and prose. True, both Updike and Lawrence have reputations as poets as well as authors of prose, and it might be argued that a poetic ear shaped their prose, but I think that a better explanation is that alternating stress is so natural to our language and so pervasive that it can be found in most passages of good writing, especially in fiction, which has more of a tendency toward strong and frequent stresses than has discursive or expository prose.

Of course the poetic form affects the way you read these passages. It makes you dwell a moment on the lines, to stress syllables you would not ordinarily stress in prose reading. Updike's "So unexpectedly ponderous was the blade" rings like a majestic line of Christopher Marlowe's when set as poetry, but is much less emphatic in its original prose paragraph. Berger's "And cool himself and clear his throat and then" is made up of ordinary words that would ripple by unnoticed in their prose paragraph, but they sing like a line of perfectly regular iambic pentameter. The passage from Lawrence strikes me as especially powerful in its pentameter form. The meter is varied, the language sonorous, and the passage much more powerful than the same words printed as prose. Listen to those rhythms:

> and it SEEMED \ she was LIKE \ the SEA, \ NOTHing \
>   but DARK \
> WAVES RIS \ ing and HEAV \ ing WITH a \
>   GREAT SWELL, \
> so that SLOW \ ly her \ WHOLE DARK \ ness WAS \ in MO \
>   tion
> and SHE \ was O \ cean ROLL \ ing its DARK \ DUMB
>   MASS.

It is worthy of W. B. Yeats! (There is one foot in the second line which is uncommon in English verse: the amphibrach, ᴗ / ᴗ .) I wish the fashion would change again, that most fiction and much discursive writing were metrical, as such material was handled in other eras. The form makes us pay more attention to language, to savor its subtleties and its music.

But metrical form is the bone structure. Let's consider the flesh. All these passages are, for instance, rich in images. **Imagery** in language causes us to imagine something concrete—usually something we can see, but the term is also used for images of sound, odor, or other things perceptible to the senses. They vary in intensity. In number 1 the word "home" is vague, not causing us to visualize much, but "flannel gown" is much more vivid. One assumes that "home" and "flannel gown" are **literal:** the speaker was, indeed, in his home and was wearing a flannel gown. The next image is **figurative:** "like a bear to its floe," is a figure of speech, in this case a **simile,** or explicit comparison. It modifies the image of "clambered." The speaker describes himself as clambering like a bear. Notice that nothing has been said about whiteness or ice or northern climates, but these images have stimulated us to think of whiteness and the icy North. We know the flannel gown is not red. After the semicolon we move into a dream, and the image "globe's impossible sides" helps create a dream atmosphere. Another figure is involved—**hyperbole,** or exaggeration. We know the sides of the globe are not literally "impossible," or the speaker could not sail up them, even in a dream. They are so steep as to seem impossible. What about "sides"? That is a **metaphor.** The curving slope of the globe is compared to something more wall-like, to convey the sense of heroic endeavor this dream involves. "Black beard," "furs," "dogs," "northern pole," all are literal images—in a special sense. He was not really there with furs and dogs, and might not really have a black beard, but this was literally what he dreamed.

Such analysis might seem ridiculously complex, but communication is always a complex phenomenon. Communication in imaginative writing, perhaps especially in poetry, is likely to be more complex than in other kinds of writing. It is amazingly condensed. The simple domestic event of going to bed to dream is transformed in these few lines into high comedy and mock-heroic high adventure. Poetic form causes us to slow down in reading, to dwell on words, to suck them of their marrow. And if you are going to write good poetry, you had better learn how to provide a reader with something worth savoring, something rewarding to that attention which poetic form invites.

We have seen images that were literal and figurative. At another level they may be symbolic. A **symbol** is anything that stands for a meaning that is unexpressed. "Black beard" symbolizes manliness, "furs" and "dogs" symbolize exploration, and, by extension, adventure and heroism. "Flannel" sounds a little old-fashioned, doesn't it? It reminds me of

"Ma in her kerchief and me in my cap" from "A Visit from St. Nicholas," symbolizing a personality that is conservative, self-protecting, perhaps even self-indulgent—a comic opposite of the bold explorer with black beard, furs, and dogs.

The heft of the scimitar in number 2 is more explicitly symbolic—in this case evoking, for the speaker, a philosophical interpretation of ultimate reality. Why does he think of an orange? That image might suggest many things about the scimitar and the experience of picking it up— perhaps the color of the bronze handle, perhaps its unexpected ponderousness, the compactness and weight of the fruit—or perhaps an orange, like the heavy sword, seems to the speaker to be a core of solidity beneath illusion, the rock in Plato's cave (where, in the philosopher's parable, all experience of the senses was represented as shadow and illusion). Since the speaker is about to use the scimitar to decapitate an old king, he might also be thinking of the orange as the head itself, so soon to roll away. In part, the effectiveness of this symbolic image is its incongruity (and rather grisly humor) in the context. Sometimes such images shimmer with undefined meaning. Incongruous images must have popped into your mind at times in the midst of intense experience. They symbolize something deep in your subconscious, something which your conscious mind probably does not grasp. Images sometimes work the same way in imaginative writing.

It may be that twentieth-century poets (influenced by Freud and Jung) have overdone the use of irrational symbols such as that orange—images whose meanings are only subconsciously grasped, if at all. This practice intimidates many readers, who conclude that symbolism is obscure, intellectual, or perversely personal. But most symbolism is quite natural and intelligible. It doesn't take much exercise of mind or imagination to associate in number 3 the dwindling fire with Uther Pendragon's diminishing potency, and the association between killing people in battle and sexual exercise is quite explicit. These images are also literal: the fire had indeed been reduced to ashes, the king was, indeed, exhausted by his labors, and since the speech to come (which I did not quote) is ironic, it is probably to be understood that the king literally put his tongue in his cheek.

The imagery in number 4 circles close around its central symbolism— the sea as symbol for the primal forces released in Lady Chatterley as she makes love. Notice that it starts with the simile "she was *like* the sea," and proceeds to a more assertive metaphor for the same comparison: "she was ocean." (**Metaphor** is the general term for such comparisons; **simile** is the kind of metaphor in which the comparison is made explicit, using the word *like* or *as*.) In this passage there is a displacement, so the sea imagery is substituted for literal imagery describing the sexual act. Of course she may also literally have been heaving and rising and swelling and rolling, but Lawrence presses us so intently to identify her experience with that of the sea that we probably do not think so much of the literal meaning as we do of the symbolic meaning. He inundates us with the sea, transmuting the physical into a spiritual experience. This is the kind of writing many describe as "poetic," even when it occurs, as here, in the midst of a prose novel.

Gardner's narrator of *Jason & Medeia* (number 5) is a modern man who witnesses the ancient myth as in a dream. The quoted passage introduces Book 3, and, like many such passages throughout the epic, serves as a transition from the mind of the narrator back into the story. Thus the imagery of the first three lines is literal; the imagery of the fourth line, figurative. Throughout this discussion, *literal* does *not* mean "factual." These are obviously imaginary events. But literal images are those which are to be understood primarily in terms of the things named, not as comparisons or as symbols for something else. They may, in addition, have a symbolic suggestiveness. A lonely man leaning against a tree in an otherwise featureless landscape, looking into an abyss, hearing a rustle of voices, might suggest in some vague way the situation of anyone attempting to understand the past, eavesdropping on human culture, awed and puzzled by ancient mysteries. We need not interpret the lines that way to enjoy the poem, but the associations are easy, natural, and appropriate, and probably the poet had some such range of feelings in mind when he chose to place the narrator in this setting to begin Book 3.

We have seen in several of these passages, perhaps most clearly in that from Lawrence, how prose writers at times infuse their writing with deliberately "poetic" effects (that is, passages which seem highly charged with imagination, rich with symbolism, richly suggestive). Conversely, poets are often deliberately prosaic—holding the reader's attention on hard fact and practical, clear communication.

I will quote the whole poem from which passage number 6 is taken,

Muriel Rukeyser's "Boy With His Hair Cut Short," so we can study in greater detail how meaning arises from images:

> Sunday shuts down on this twentieth-century evening.
> The L passes. Twilight and bulb define
> the brown room, the overstuffed plum sofa,
> the boy, and the girl's thin hands above his head.
> A neighbor's radio sings stocks, news, serenade.
>
> He sits at the table, head down, the young clear neck exposed,
> watching the drugstore sign from the tail of his eye;
> tattoo, neon, until the eye blears, while his
> solicitous tall sister, simple in blue, bending
> behind him, cuts his hair with her cheap shears.
>
> The arrow's electric red always reaches its mark,
> successful neon! He coughs, impressed by that precision.
> His child's forehead, forever protected by his cap,
> is bleached against the lamplight as he turns head
> and steadies to let the snippets drop.
>
> Erasing the failure of weeks with level fingers,
> she sleeks the fine hair, combing: "You'll look fine tomorrow!
> You'll surely find something, they can't keep turning you down;
> the finest gentleman's not so trim as you!" Smiling, he raises
> the adolescent forehead wrinkling ironic now.
>
> He sees his decent suit laid out, new-pressed,
> his carfare on the shelf. He lets his head fall, meeting
> her earnest hopeless look, seeing the sharp blades splitting,
> the darkened room, the impersonal sign, her motion,
> the blue vein on her temple, pitifully beating.

Even in this relatively simple, straightforward poem, various kinds of imagery, symbolism, points of view, and shifts in language interweave to convey a complex experience. Meaning arises from the whole poem, transcending literal statement or simple paraphrase.

She sets her characters in a hard, clear light—like figures in a Vermeer painting. Most of the images are literal, unadorned. Are "head down" in the second stanza and "lets his head fall" in the last symbolic of defeat? Does the flashing tattoo of the drugstore neon arrow symbolize cheap, gaudy success? Probably—but these overtones seem almost distractions from the simple clarity of the images.

There are actually three characters in the poem: the boy, the girl, and the poet, the last an almost invisible presence. It is as though Rukeyser were recording the scene with a documentary camera, but there are some clues to her attitudes creeping in, like the word "solicitous" in the second stanza. Who sees the girl as solicitous? Who says the radio of the neighbor "sings" stocks and news? These are subjective words of the poet, interpreting, not just presenting the evidence. Of course there is a subtle subjectivity in each decision as to which details to present, where to point the camera. The poet may have overlooked a bottle of gin on the sink, or doughnuts of rolled hose on the bathroom floor—details another poet might pick up to express a different interpretation of the scene.

Who regards the flashing arrow on the sign as "successful neon!"? We know from the remainder of the stanza that we are being given glimpses into the mind of the boy, though the language ("impressed by that precision") may be more the poet's than his. Who calls his forehead a "child's"? That is the poet again, slipping in a judgment, though still remaining close to objectivity. She backs the judgment with explanation and evidence: the forehead is pale and unlined, "forever protected by his cap." The detail enables us to imagine a little of the childhood so newly past, the bill of the cap pulled low over the small face. (Notice, by the way, the line of tetrameter closing the third stanza; the pentameter of the rest of the poem is loose, sometimes stretching to six feet.)

Is the sister literally "Erasing the failure of weeks with level fingers"? No, she is cutting hair, not erasing anything. The language is figurative, but with a twist. It is *as though* she were erasing, but not quite that, either, more as though she were *trying* to erase. To know what she is trying to do, we have to be inside her mind for a moment, preparing us for her speech. It is the camera again which sees him smile and raise his head, that sees his forehead wrinkle, but the poet interprets it as "adolescent" and "ironic." Why the shift from "child's forehead" in the preceding stanza to "adolescent forehead" here? I think the irony is the explanation. The boy smiles at his sister's speech, but not in total acceptance. In the next stanza he will be looking into her "hopeless" eyes. He knows his chances are slight, in spite of her efforts to trim him up. Irony is not a child's perception. He is aging before our eyes.

Who says the suit is "decent"? That sounds like another judgment by the poet, but it tells us a great deal about the values of the boy and girl, too. We can imagine their concern about what he wears—that it not be too flashy; that it be laundered and patched, if not new; that it be the most respectable clothing available under poor circumstances. The camera picks up carfare, and we see the carefully counted coins, knowing they are a budgeted portion of a slim reserve. I assume that he "lets his head fall" after smiling so she can cut again, but I find the imagery a little awkward here—the fallen head "meeting / her earnest hopeless look" and observing the room, the sign, the blades, and the vein on her temple from that position. Were it my poem I would revise and straighten this out. Who sees her look as "earnest hopeless"? Presumably the boy—but the poet, too. It is the poet who regards the room as "darkened." (It might, objectively, be dark, but the past participle implies a choice, an act, that probably did not happen.) It is the poet's language that describes the sign as "impersonal." Above all, it is the poet who regards the beating of the girl's vein as pitiful.

In the last stanza the poem veers slightly toward propaganda, toward the social-protest poster art of the Depression era of the thirties. Is it too much? Do you feel the poet is trying to manipulate your emotions, to write a tearjerker or arouse your political feelings about social injustice? Such are the questions of taste and purpose a poet must weigh in choosing words and tactics.

I think the poem works very well—and I especially admire the last line. Imagine an alternative: "the blue vein on her temple softly pulsing." What has been lost? "Pitifully beating" suggests to me something inside, pounding to get out. I see it as symbolic of their situation, especially that of the boy. As he moves toward adult awareness he is seeing more and more clearly that the world outside with its thundering L, flashing gaudy symbols of success, and singing radios can crush the tender private lives within the apartment. The camera's eyes become the boy's eyes, recording the evidence, putting it together, grasping its meaning as he increasingly sees his own life and that of his sister as a pitiful beating in confinement. The focus on that delicate detail in the last line brings the internal and external points of view together.

The poem is multidimensional, as are the characters in it. We see the boy and girl in the round, almost hear their breathing, feel their anxieties and doubts. I have seen photographs which convey as much in so little a space—and this poem, indeed, resembles a photograph, or a documentary film. A flaw—such as, in my judgment, the word "darkened"—shows up precisely because the poem has been so effective in creating a standard of objectivity. We don't want the intrusion of the poet's judgment and feelings, though we appreciate the compassionate observation, the loving accuracy of the portrayal.

This is not, of course, the only kind of poetry which can be effective. For contrast we might look at another arising from a similar social consciousness and political concern. Edwin Markham's "The Man with the Hoe" was inspired by Millet's painting with that title. After the poem appeared in January 1899 in the *San Francisco Examiner,* it was reprinted to popular acclaim in paper after paper all over the world. The poem is said to have earned the poet over $250,000 in his lifetime, surely some kind of a record for a poem. And it is a poem of strident social protest, calling for nothing less than worldwide revolution. Its form, like that of Muriel Rukeyser's, is blank verse. Here is the first verse paragraph:

> Bowed by the weight of centuries he leans
> Upon his hoe and gazes on the ground,
> The emptiness of ages in his face,
> And on his back the burden of the world.
> Who made him dead to rapture and despair,
> A thing that grieves not and that never hopes,
> Stolid and stunned, a brother to the ox?
> Who loosened and let down this brutal jaw?
> Whose was the hand that slanted back this brow?
> Whose breath blew out the light within his brain?

Markham's method is almost the opposite of Rukeyser's. This is poetry of statement. The images are secondary to the author's point of view. Readers might be familiar with the painting and draw imagery from that. From the poem itself we can infer that a peasant is standing in a field, leaning on a hoe, that his face is empty, that his jaw is slack, his brow sloped. The remainder of the verse paragraph conveys the questions and implied attitudes of the poet—and the remaining four verse paragraphs (all between eight and eleven lines long) have even less imagery, more rhetoric and argument and subjective opinion.

Whereas Rukeyser's poem resembles the art of photography, Markham's draws upon the art of oratory. It is a poem to be delivered from a platform by an impassioned performer with booming voice. Rukeyser wants to give us the facts, to stir our feelings and shape our attitudes by giving us carefully chosen documentary evidence, letting us seem to make up our own minds and interpretations, with minimal guidance from the few judgment words we noted. Rukeyser's is a tactic more appealing to the tastes of our times. But, correspondingly, we have lost the appreciation for sonority and eloquence that made Markham's poem so powerful for readers at the turn of the century.

The next two verse paragraphs are devoted to the failure of the divine and human dream represented by the figure of the man—with lines such as these:

> What gulfs between him and the seraphim!
> Slave of the wheel of labor, what to him
> Are Plato and the swing of Pleiades?
> What the long reaches of the peaks of song,
> The rift of dawn, the reddening of the rose?

And though the method is mainly one of asking rhetorical questions, the answers are stated with increasingly strong language. It was "the world's blind greed" which created this "danger to the universe." The man has been "betrayed, / Plundered, profaned, and disinherited," and his shape "Cries protest to the Judges of the World." In the final two verse paragraphs the speaker addresses directly those whom he finds responsible: "O masters, lords and rulers in all lands." He asks them:

> How will the Future reckon with this man?
> How answer his brute question in that hour
> When whirlwinds of rebellion shake all shores?

The threat and the warning are explicit. Make such a speech today and you will be arrested for inciting a riot.

Or ignored. Audiences in the past seem to have had more appetite for being lectured to than we have today. This is a factor you should take into consideration as you write your own poems. What will be your stance as a poet? Are you setting yourself up as a lecturer, telling people what they ought to think and feel? How does that affect your language, the kinds of imagery you use, your tone? If you were in the audience (instead of on the platform), would you listen? Would you get up and walk out? I have read many poems by amateurs which I am certain the poets themselves would not sit still for had it been someone else unloading their feelings, opinions, and attitudes. I personally love the ringing lines of Markham's poem, as I do the rattling didacticism of Pope or the fandangos of fantastic imagery of Shakespeare's lovers or the tortured pieties of the "metaphysical" poets of the seventeenth century. But I am certain those poetic techniques would not be effective in contemporary poetry. One of the qualities of sensibility that you have to cultivate as a poet is a sensitivity to your own times, your own culture. (That does not mean you need follow slavishly the prevailing fashions, but you do need to be sensitive and responsive to the values of your readers.) Much can be gleaned from poetry of the past which has refreshing applicability to modern poetry (as I hope this book has shown). But you cannot live in or write for another age. Willy-nilly, you are a modern poet. And if you try to write as Markham did in "The Man with the Hoe," some might find you quaint, but most would find you a bore.

Analyze the imagery and symbolism in some of your own poems now. To what extent do you let literal images, photographic realism, convey the feeling and thought? Where do you see your own voice intruding with imaginative decoration, judgment, or subjective response? Is it effective, or does it detract from your purposes? How much symbolic weight do your images have? Do they suggest a larger meaning than that of mere statement? Is it clear enough for a reader to get it? Does it arise naturally from the material of the poem, or do symbols seem to be stuck in for effect?

You probably do not ordinarily write poetry of statement, such as Markham's "The Man with the Hoe," but you might try it experimentally. If you study his images (such as "The peaks of song, / The rift of dawn, the reddening of the rose") you see how they illustrate or strengthen the statement but do not convey the primary meaning of the poem as Rukeyser's images do. Try using images this way, emphasizing the clarity and power of the sentence, rendering the sentence more eloquent with images and figures of speech. Notice that poetry of statement works only in a strong metrical (probably accentual syllabic) framework. It quickly falls flat when the medium is free verse, or even a meter as loose as Rukeyser's. Why is that? By now this book should have supplied you with some answers.

Poetry of statement can never be *mere* statement, nor can any good poetry. That is, something else is always going on, in every line, in addition to simple conveyance of meaning. It may be meter or rhyme or sound manipulation, but most commonly (in addition to these), it is imagery. Whole poems without images are rare, and those such as Frost's "Home Burial," studied in Chapter 11, which are relatively barren of imagery and yet effective, are rare indeed. It is a challenge to try to keep a poem so near the edge of statement and yet make it sing. But generally you will find literal, figurative, and symbolic images providing the main substance for your poetry.

They are certainly the first thing noticed by most readers. Often we hand a friend a copy of one of our poems and get the response (after puzzled silence), "Well, I like the images." Our hearts sink. In spite of all the positive things I have said about them, images are also the geegaws of poetry. They stand out, strike the eye, and that is good to some extent. But we are disappointed if they have so held a reader's attention that he failed to see the poem's larger purposes, its structure, direction, and meaning. We want readers to notice the wall, not just the pictures hanging on it. We want them to see, at least, how the pictures relate to one another, how they fit into a complex of purpose. When the only response our poems get is a vacuous approval of their images, we know we still have work to do.

Using images well is like using any other element of poetry. You don't want them to run away with the poem. You need to keep them under control, sometimes harmoniously fitting together, at other times deliberately in violent juxtaposition. They tend to be so powerful, so noticeable, that they sometimes convey meanings or associations you never intended, sometimes at cross-purposes to your intentions. If you tell a sweetheart, "I love you as a pig loves mud," you might fail to convey the sincerity and tenderness you meant, though in your private view a pig's love of mud is quite sincere and tender.

Your best guidance is studying, as we studied the imagery of Rukeyser's poem, the imagery of poetry you admire. Image by image.

How does each work? How does each fit with the others? How does each move the poem along? Then look again at your own poems and see whether you learned anything.

14

Into the Maelstrom

Sensationalism in Modern Poetry

So far I have tried to help you write better poetry. This chapter is (with the same intent) a warning. If you read much of the poetry published today in quality and literary magazines, you may find many examples of poems which are incomprehensible, even unreadable. You may believe that your own intelligence or taste or background is at fault. After all, if respected editors chose to print these poems, you might think, the poems must have *some* excellence. You may feel put down and insulted by what you see in modern poetry, fiction, drama, art, and music. You are reacting to a quality I call sensationalism, which I will define and illustrate here. You may want to *follow* such models as I will provide, and following them may, indeed, help you get your poems published, for sensationalism is very fashionable. But I call the chapter a warning because I believe such writing, which alienates so many readers, is in the long run unhealthy for poetry and literature.

Here is a poem one would never mistake for prose. It is the title poem of the second and major volume by Sylvia Plath, one of the most highly esteemed poets of our century. The book appeared after her suicide in 1965:

Ariel

Stasis in darkness.
Then the substanceless blue
Pour of tor and distances.

God's lioness,
How one we grow,
Pivot of heels and knees!—The furrow

Splits and passes, sister to
The brown arc
Of the neck I cannot catch,

Nigger-eye
Berries cast dark
Hooks—

Black sweet blood mouthfuls,
Shadows.
Something else

Hauls me through air—
Thighs, hair;
Flakes from my heels.

White
Godiva, I unpeel—
Dead hands, dead stringencies.

And now I
Foam to wheat, a glitter of seas.
The child's cry

Melts in the wall.
And I
Am the arrow,

The dew that flies
Suicidal, at one with the drive
Into the red

Eye, the cauldron of morning.

Plath was a brilliant, gifted poet, and many of her poems (such as "Fever 103°" discussed in Chapter 12) are powerful and clear, luminous even in their psychotic extravagance. And since much analysis and explication of her work has appeared, I am sure there is an explanation of "Ariel" (the name of her favorite horse) in some academic critique. But I am also sure the poem makes no sense. One might study it, as a psychiatrist might analyze the doodling of a mental patient for insights into madness, for a better understanding of the woman. But its value as art for any sort of general audience is questionable.

This might be regarded as an exceptional case, a fascinating perversion of a sadly deranged genius, except that you can open almost any contemporary literary magazine and find examples of poems which make no more sense than this, though they will probably be less sensational in imagery, less skillful in management of sound and formal elements. How did poetry get into such a state? Why do editors publish things that neither they nor their readers can possibly understand?

Part of the problem is an association of the content of poetry with images, phrases, and individual words rather than with sentences. (Robert Frost called his act of writing poetry "sentencing," a view which might be a healthy corrective for our times.) Transitions are abandoned. All the little connectives and business words are squeezed out. The effort is to capture the flamy dance of imagination (that is, the capacity for making images) rather than coherent patterns of thought or conversational ease of speech. There are, indeed, sentences in "Ariel," and other groups of words are punctuated as sentences but can't be read as sentences. Imagine finding in prose something like "—The furrow splits and passes, sister to the brown arc of the neck I cannot catch, nigger-eye berries cast dark hooks—black sweet blood mouthfuls, shadows." The computer has short-circuited.

The poems by Rukeyser and Markham we looked at in the last chapter are both examples of "sentencing." Though Rukeyser communicates primarily by images, she hangs the images on coherent sentences in a clear narrative. Markham develops a rational argument and expresses feelings and judgments, using occasional images to make the argument more vivid. But the poetic method which, at its extreme, results in poems such as Sylvia Plath's "Ariel" is of another sort entirely. In this kind, the narrative or logical structure is suppressed, or made secondary to the images. One of the best-known poems of this sort—which also happens to argue in favor of its aesthetic principles—is Archibald MacLeish's "Ars Poetica" (the title means, "the art of poetry"):

A poem should be palpable and mute
As a globed fruit.

Dumb
As old medallions to the thumb,

Silent as the sleeve-worn stone
Of casement ledges where the moss has grown.

A poem should be wordless
As the flights of birds.

*

A poem should be motionless in time
As the moon climbs,

Leaving, as the moon releases
Twig by twig the night-entangled trees,

Leaving, as the moon behind the winter leaves
Memory by memory the mind—

A poem should be motionless in time
As the moon climbs.

*

A poem should be equal to:
Not true.

For all the history of grief
An empty doorway and a maple leaf.

For love
The leaning grasses and two lights above the sea—

A poem should not mean
But be.

There are, indeed, coherent sentences throughout. It is a poem that can "mean" and "be" at the same time. But to understand it you have to dwell on the images, one by one, to let them sink in, and to make some connections between them in your mind.

How can a poem be mute, dumb, silent, wordless—the adjectives in the first section? I think he must mean the poem should avoid abstractions, that it should speak primarily to the senses, not the intellect. But the very adjectives chosen are abstractions. We wouldn't have a clue as to what he meant by globed fruit or old medallions, and so on, without those abstractions—or without the opening injunction: "A poem should be. . . ." But we cannot get the full sense from the abstractions without the images. Think of a fruit, like a globe, something round, firm, silent, something you can touch, hold in your hand. A poem cannot be that exactly, but it can be *like* that—and, for me at least, this poem is. I see it, feel it, hold it, letting its thought come through my fingers as though I were rubbing an ancient coin (or medallion) with my eyes closed, sensing its long history of being rubbed by thumbs. Think of a stone sill of a castle window, eroded by a thousand years of contact with silken sleeves of lonely maidens, the moss of ages worn away by such delicate contact. A poem should (this poem says) somehow be like that, durable, embodying the emotional history of all who have felt its surfaces. I am by now imaginatively in that castle; I am that lonely maiden. I have fondled a fruit in the slant of sun through the open window. I have rubbed the king's face on a coin. I have carried my melancholy to the window to look down. A covey of birds whirs up from the garden below, wordless, with heart-stopping suddenness and grace. The poem did not tell that story: it welled up in me through silent contact with the images. A somewhat different chain of associations might arise in your mind, but they would circle around the core of the poem's implied statement. The poem is helping you feel (rather than explicitly understand) what MacLeish thinks a poem should be.

The motion of bird flight is immediately turned into another paradox:

the poem should be motionless. But motionless in what way? As the moon climbs. Motionless motion. It does not seem to move, but it moves. Or, more precisely, the world moves, creating the sense of its climbing. Are we still at that casement, watching the night, watching the twigs, one by one, becoming distinct in the climbing light? Not necessarily, but maybe: something like that. What has this to do with poetry? This poem you just read has not changed, has not spoken, but twig by twig it is becoming clearer. Where has the motion come from? Your world is turning, time eroding the stone sills, understanding seeping in. The first couplet of the second section is repeated. The poem is going round and round, staying still.

The third section, then, risks two abstractions in its first and final couplet. No images. But the assertion is that the flesh of the poem is, indeed, images, symbols—conveying the abstraction of grief through the concrete images of an empty doorway and a maple leaf, the abstraction of love through images of leaning grass and two lights above the sea.

If the poem were to take its own advice too literally, the last section might be reduced to an empty doorway and a maple leaf, leaning grasses and two lights above the sea—and we would have to guess that the poet was talking about grief and love, and about poetry. Some poets of the early part of this century did, indeed, squeeze all abstractions out. It was a very narrow interpretation of what poetry should be—one that would exclude most of Homer, Dante, Goethe, Chaucer, Shakespeare, Milton, Pope, Browning, Yeats, Frost (and most of MacLeish's own work). But it was a powerful and influential argument and still, in one form or another, governs the practice of many poets today. MacLeish, of course, was never such a fanatic. This is not an Imagist poem. For me its beauty (and it is one of the most beautiful poems I know) has much to do with its form: those limber couplets playing the line lengths against one another from monometer to hexameter, the careful structure of four couplets to a section, the deeply woven rhymes and rich sound texture. I also love its images and am much attracted by its meaning (much as I disagree with it as a general prescription for the art of poetry), though meaning is the quality the poem explicitly says a poem should not have. But without its element of statement it would be a mere jumble of sensuous impressions.

That is what we saw in Sylvia Plath's "Ariel." Go back and read it again. From the title I would assume it is about disembodied imagination, the spirit of poetry, about being carried away. From that brown arc of neck I would guess she imagines herself on a horse, maybe one with the horse. Pegasus? No, she is Lady Godiva. What that has to do with eating blackberries I am not sure. As the mother is carried away by her poetry, she apparently neglects her baby. Obviously her poetic impulse is suicidal: she wants to dissolve in the dawn like the dew.

And because she was, in fact, suicidal, the imagery has great sensational force. Our attention has been turned from the poem to the woman, from the art to the person. Maybe that is what she wanted. Her poems often seem like cries of desperation, like the cryptic notes psychotics leave in wild hope that someone will find them out, stop them, cure them. How many poems do you find in the literary magazines which are similarly exhibitionistic, cries for attention, as though poets were saying you must listen to me *because* I make no sense. I am either crazy or inspired—in any case a rather special person, not to be judged by ordinary standards.

I have used, without defining, the word *sensationalism* because the ordinary meaning of the word, as given in a dictionary, is sufficient to tell you what I mean. My Webster's defines *sensational* as: "arousing or tending to arouse (as by lurid details) a quick, intense, and usually superficial interest, curiosity, or emotional reaction." One meaning of *sensationalism* is philosophical: "empiricism that limits experience as a source of knowledge to sensation or sense perception." The word *sensation* in this definition means "a mental process (as seeing, hearing, or smelling) due to immediate bodily stimulation often as distinguished from awareness of the process." The whole range of meanings given in the dictionary for these words conveys a sense (or sensation?) of what has been going on in modern art, including poetry, since the first decade of our century.

It is an understandable response to our cultural turmoil. Since the eighteenth century, philosophers had been wrestling intently with the question of how we know what we know, and many had concluded that all awareness was ultimately based upon sense data—sensations. We have (they argued) no fixed ideas given us at birth, distinguishing our humanity. Our reasoning is rationalization, not a path to truth. Our faith is illusion. We know nothing except by experience, and experience consists of nothing but the information of our senses. Perhaps there is nothing, really, out there to be sensed. All we know is that we sense.

Varieties of such thought, both at the philosophical and popular levels, were a response to ideological conflict, relativism, decline of belief in conventional religions or other claims to explanations of reality. In poetry, images were the verbal counterparts of sensations. Japanese poetry became influential because it eschewed generalization and moralizing; to early twentieth-century intellectuals in the Western world it seemed to consist of pure images, with all abstraction removed. An influential poem of the first decades of our century (published in 1917) was Wallace Stevens's "Thirteen Ways of Looking at a Blackbird." It is, like MacLeish's "Ars Poetica," a poem I love. Here are the first three of its thirteen strophes:

I

Among twenty snowy mountains,
The only moving thing
Was the eye of the blackbird.

II

I was of three minds,
Like a tree
In which there are three blackbirds.

III

The blackbird whirled in the autumn winds.
It was a small part of the pantomime.

Each of the thirteen strophes mentions a blackbird or blackbirds, but there is otherwise no unity in the poem. The strophes are not in any necessary order. Stevens said of the poem that it was really a collection of thirteen independent poems, inspired by Japanese haiku, and the stanzas could be arranged in any order. In stanza 7 he mentions "Haddam":

O thin men of Haddam,
Why do you imagine golden birds?
Do you not see how the blackbird
Walks around the feet
Of the women about you?

Sounds rather biblical, doesn't it? But Haddam is a town in Connecticut, the state in which Stevens lived. He used it because he liked the sound of it. Why are the men thin? He liked the sound. Why shouldn't they imagine golden birds, even though a blackbird walks around the feet of the women? No reason. It is a sensational contrast.

Thoughtlessness was an end in itself. The images frustrate and prohibit thinking. They defy "rational" expectations of logic, order, coherence, significance. The poem is a Zen-like search for freedom from the busy noise of the mind. It is not about looking at a blackbird, one way or thirteen ways. It is about nothing. The very word "about" insults its purity. It is a creation of words as a painting is a creation of paints. Pictures were, increasingly, no longer pictures *of* a subject. They were not *about* anything. They were to be valued for themselves alone, without any reference to things outside themselves. Poetry was moving in that direction.

Another poem published in 1917 is one of my favorites of all times, one which has had as much to do with forming me as a poet as any other single poem: T. S. Eliot's "The Love Song of J. Alfred Prufrock." Its opening lines grab attention like a headline:

> Let us go then, you and I,
> When the evening is spread out against the sky
> Like a patient etherised upon a table.

I hope I do not seem unappreciative of the beauty and power of this poem when I say these lines make no sense. For one thing (and this may be merely picky), the first line is ungrammatical. "You and I" is in apposition to "us," and so it should be "you and me," the way it would be said colloquially. That "I" is putting on airs, language trying to be genteel; it gives its artificiality away by being ungrammatical.

But how can an evening be spread out against the sky like a patient etherised upon a table? It is fanciful to think of the evening as separate from the sky and spread out against it. That is a metaphor tangled enough to begin with. But there is no way one can visualize an evening as a patient. Is a patient spread out "against" a table? The image is neither graceful nor vivid, but it is certainly sensational. Whoever thought of comparing an evening to a patient etherised on a table? No one, before Eliot (and for good reason). The clinical word "etherised" was startling.

Such language hadn't often been used in poetry.

Who are "you and I" anyway? "I," one assumes, is Prufrock. But there is no auditor in the poem (which is a dramatic monologue). He is talking to himself. He calls himself "you." (Eliot claimed that he meant Prufrock to be speaking to an unnamed companion, but the poem makes no sense except as reverie.) I have read ingenious critical explanations of each of these points, rationalizations even for the bad grammar, but I think efforts to "explain" the poem are missing the poet's own point.

Toward the end of the poem are these lines:

I grow old . . I grow old. . .
I shall wear the bottoms of my trousers rolled.

Why rolled? I always assumed it was because he is talking about walking along the beach, and he didn't want to get them wet. But when T. S. Eliot was teaching a seminar at the University of Chicago, one of his students had a different interpretation. "Mr. Eliot," he asked, "is Prufrock thinking that when he gets old his body will shrink, and that's why he will roll up his trousers?" Eliot looked bemused. He said, "Why, I suppose it might mean that. I never thought of it." Eliot explicitly said that one needn't understand a poem to appreciate it, that he often appreciated poetry which he didn't understand for years, or in some cases never came to understand, including some of Shakespeare. He was not, even as early as "Prufrock," writing to be understood. He was writing works of art—and art was meant, not to be understood, but to be appreciated.

That is the cultural climate you must cope with as a poet. It is a cultural climate in which people grow accustomed to walking by examples of modern painting or sculpture, or to hearing modern music without looking for or expecting any human connection, any relevance to their lives. It is not polite to ask what art is about or to ask that it be melodic or moving or memorable. The same sophisticated indifference carries over to poetry. One simply accepts incomprehensibility as though it were an indication of quality. Art thus becomes decoration, a kind of screaming wallpaper. Music becomes blended into the background noise of industrial society. And poetry is, like particle physics, or graphs, or economic indices, a gray blur, intended, presumably, for specialists.

We began with the question of how such a poem as Sylvia Plath's "Ariel" could be not only published but admired and celebrated, though it plainly makes no sense. Much of the explanation for the state of mind which produces and encourages such poetry is the assumption that the content of poetry is different by nature from that of prose. Poetry is an arrangement of images and symbols, with emphasis on individual words, figures of speech, overtones, clusters of lurid details, rather than on sentences and coherent development of thought or presentation of experience. Because our sense of form has been undermined by the prevalence of free verse, poets increasingly depend upon startling or obscure or sensational content to make their writing seem poetic. The result is frantic juxtaposing of verbal baubles on strings of broken lines.

I hope you will not be lured, looking for intellectual approval, into that state of mind. As I have mentioned before, the modernist movement in poetry began in an effort to bring to poetry a wider audience. The sensationalism of Carl Sandburg's "Chicago" or of Vachel Lindsay's "The Congo" (Remember that one? "Boomlay, boomlay, boomlay, boom . . .") was successful in doing just that. It sold poetry to people who had no interest in it before.

At the same time, however, poets in an industrialized society yearned for an aristocratic position, not by birth but by sensitivity. The motto of *Transition*, the literary magazine which first published much of James Joyce's *Ulysses*, was "the common reader be damned." The stance of the poet was that of a person apart, one who could not possibly be understood by the blue-collar, lunch-box masses. Most of the modernist poets wrote criticism as well, putting together among them an elitist aesthetic, boosting one another, helping one another to prizes, grants, publication, and recognition. The emphasis was upon being erudite, difficult, and beyond thought. Explanation of life was the business of scientists. The poets spoke of a separate reality, one presumably known only to them, one which they recognized in one another's work. In the process we have lost our readership. Ask anyone, including yourself, to name ten living American poets, and I predict you will encounter stumbling and hesitation or blank silence.

Another problem with sensationalism is that it is a continually changing style. If the same effect is repeated too often, it is no longer sensational. Styles of poetry have, consequently, succeeded one another like waves of fashion. Where are the miniskirts of yesteryear? A favorite word of criticism has come to be "strange." A poem is appreciated because it is "new," or "fresh." Fashion is full of paradoxes. In mid-career, Robert Lowell discovered the power—believe it or not—of direct statement, especially about himself, especially about embarrassing things about himself. (Remember, in "Skunk Hour," quoted in Chapter 9, the line "My mind's not right"? What a blockbuster that was!) The fashion of "confessional" poetry was in vogue for a decade.

This is cocktail-party culture. The resulting poetry does not reach and has no concern with ordinary readers. In this book I have tried to ignore all that, and I hope you have the strength to ignore it as a poet. Rather, I am concerned with durable goods, with the qualities that characterize the excellent poetry of the ancient Greeks as much as that of today. It wasn't until modern times that the word *modern* was used as a term of approval or praise. Its sense was closer to *modish,* implying merely fashionable, temporary, of no lasting interest or value, as when the "Justice" is described in Shakespeare's *As You Like It* as being "Full of wise saws and modern instances." As a poet or a person, you can't help being modern. That is an accident of birth. The question is, can you be anything else? I hope this book helps you, as it has helped me, at least to aim at goals of more enduring value.

15

In and Out of the Closet

Finding an Audience; Publication

Once you have all these fine poems written, what do you do with them? Emily Dickinson got ahead by storing most of hers in her trunk—and I know many poets who are following the same route in hope of immortality. Poetry is a lonely art, offering little reward in fame or fortune, as I will explain in this chapter. But before discouraging you, I will try to answer some of the common questions beginners have.

First you probably want an audience—someone besides your family and friends, preferably someone who might respond both sympathetically and critically, appreciating the strengths in your work and helping you overcome your weaknesses, at least by pointing out what doesn't seem to work. Such an audience is hard to find: I have rarely had one myself. But you are most likely to find it in a writers' group or workshop.

Find out if there is a chapter of your state poetry society which meets in your vicinity (by writing the National Society of State Poetry Societies, 1121 Major Ave. NW, Albuquerque, NM 87107). Ask around (for example, at the library, at any nearby college or university) to locate other groups. Or start your own! For example, you might take out an ad in a local paper asking writers (or specifically poets) to get in touch with you for the purpose of forming a group. You might want to attend one of the dozens of workshops given around the country every year, advertised in *Writer's Digest*. Perhaps you could take a course in creative writing, such as universities often offer through their extension programs or those given at local community centers, Golden Age centers, libraries, or other adult-education facilities (and you don't technically have to be an adult to participate in most). In cities and university communities there are often coffeehouses, bookstores, or other settings in which informal poetry readings are given. Attend, get acquainted, and see whether you can find the nucleus of a group to meet on a regular basis.

What makes such a group work is the willingness of each to trade attention and criticism for the same in return; but in spite of good intentions, the discussion is often frustrating and impressionistic. It might help if the group were to study together a text such as this book to focus disagreements and provide some common background regarding fundamentals. Each poet (or writer) should provide enough carbons or photocopies of work to be discussed so that each person in the group can have a copy to look at. Practice reading your work aloud—and it helps, too, to trade off, to take turns reading one another's work aloud, so that you can find out whether the sounds and rhythms and emotional expression you think you put into the manuscript are actually there or remain in your head. Many such groups offer prizes or competitions, and there are many national prizes offered by the National Society of State Poetry Societies. These provide a way to test the effectiveness of your work outside your local group.

When I began thinking of submitting my work for publication, I had just finished reading a book by the critic Edmund Wilson, who had a reputation for discovering new writers. I sent him several of my poems, with a flattering letter—and the batch came back, several months later, with a severe printed card saying Edmund Wilson does not do a whole list of things (and reading amateur poetry was one of them) except for a fee. That was a more personal response than you will get from most well-known writers, who will simply ignore such correspondence. Now that I have some reputation, I get hundreds of such packets a year, and answer them with a printed refusal. Don't waste your time. It isn't as though well-known writers are heartless or mercenary: it is simply impossible to open oneself to a flood of such requests and have any time for one's own work.

For much more detailed (and encouraging) advice on seeking publication, as well as descriptions of thousands of markets, see the annual

Poet's Market: Where and How to Publish Your Poetry. The suggestions which follow apply to most, but not all, publishers. If you want to submit poetry for publication in magazines (I'll come to books later), face it, you are on your own. Do not fall for the advertisements of "agents" or others who say they are willing to read your work and place it. They are after your money. Reputable agents simply do not handle poetry; there isn't enough money in it to make it worth their while. (Occasionally as a sideline agents may handle the poetry written by successful prose writers, but they earn their commissions on the prose, not the poetry.) Go to the library (a university library if one is available to you) and read the poetry in literary magazines. You might find some in avant-garde or literary bookstores, too, though not in the chain bookstores such as you find in shopping malls. Subscribe to, or buy sample copies of, those magazines which interest you. You are looking for your level, for the magazines which reflect the taste and skill and values you share. Ask yourself, can I imagine my poems in this magazine? If the editors like what they have published here, would they be likely to respond to my poems? Read the editorial statements, usually published on the page with the masthead, to find out how (and whether) to submit.

In general, your poems should be typed, no more than one to a page, usually double-spaced, on 8-1/2 x 11″ paper, your name and address on each poem (as the packet will be shuffled around, and you don't want your poems lost on the editor's desk). Keep a carbon (and careful records of where your poems have been sent). Proofread carefully—and if you are weak in spelling, grammar, or usage, get help. (I have often had to advise beginning poets that they need to study basic English before they begin thinking of professional submission.) The poem as submitted should be exactly as you would like to see it appear, down to the last comma and capital. Editors tend to be very impatient with careless or illiterate manuscripts, especially of poetry. Submit three to five pages of poetry in a packet. Always enclose a self-addressed stamped envelope (SASE), or you may get no reply at all. A covering letter is not necessary—and you should not include one unless you have something of substance to say. In any case, keep it brief, a business letter, sticking to facts. Don't try to tell the editor how good these poems are or how he or she should interpret them. Let the editor find out.

Let me say a word about titles. Most poems, of course, have titles, and those which do not are referred to by their first lines, which then, in effect, become their titles. Avoid titles that are mere abstractions, such as "Courage," or "Love," or "Infidelity." Those sound like the titles of essays (and not essays that many would want to read!). A good title of a poem is part of the experience of the poem, not a label for it. It may not at first make sense to a reader, but at some critical point in the poem the significance of the title should become clear. A fairly common practice is to use some image or phrase or variation of one of these for the title, so the title will echo in the reader's mind when he encounters it in the poem.

Your title should be typed plainly, without quotation marks unless it is a quotation from another writer, at the top of the page. Your name and address will probably be at the upper right-hand corner. Some poets put the line count at the top of the page, but that is unnecessary, as are all such pseudoprofessional phrases as "First North American Serial Rights Only." You do not need to copyright your poem before submitting it. It will be copyrighted with the whole magazine by the editors (in most cases), and if you want to use it again, for a collection or some other purpose, write to the magazine and ask to have the copyright transferred to you—which is usually done without question (and, of course, without fee).

I have been talking primarily about the literary magazines and quality general magazines (such as *Atlantic*, or *The New Yorker*). If you don't identify with or like the poetry in magazines such as these, you might do better to explore church magazines, popular women's magazines, pulps, and other markets. Or it may be that your verse is suitable for greeting cards. These popular markets usually pay much better than the quality markets, but the poetry which appears in them is not held in high critical esteem. You couldn't care less—if you are a popular poet. Find the audience and the media appropriate to your talents and interests and forget about the literary world. In each case, study the market carefully before submitting. For example, if you are interested in freelancing greeting cards, study the cards on the stands, noting which varieties come from which companies. Take down the addresses of the companies and write (with a SASE) to inquire whether they are interested in freelance submissions and, if so, whether they have tip sheets regarding their current needs. Some newspapers have poetry columns—and instructions for submission are usually given. Wherever you see the kind of poetry you like and think you can write, explore the possibilities and find out the proper methods of submission.

In any case, do not respond to advertisements asking for poetry. There are dozens of "vanity" gimmicks for exploiting beginning poets— contests turn out to be lures for anthologies which accept your poetry only if you buy an expensive anthology. (If you fall for this, you may be sure that all the other poets in the printed volume will be suckers like yourself.) Sometimes "Poems Wanted" ads are from people who will offer to put your work to music and market it for a fee. There are a hundred variations on these schemes to fleece unsuspecting poets, and you can usually detect them by the flattery that accompanies their correspondence. If you want to stay abreast of contests of genuine literary merit and of publishing opportunities in general, you should subscribe to *Coda: Poets & Writers Newsletter,* 201 W. 54th St., New York, NY 10019. This is an informative and worthwhile periodical that serves writers in the same way that the *Wall Street Journal* serves businessmen.

You will almost never get criticism on your rejection slips. Editors have far too many submissions to deal with to open themselves to much correspondence with poets. When a packet of poems comes back from one magazine, send it out to another (having determined by studying the magazine that your kind of poetry is an appropriate submission). Don't send the same poem to more than one magazine at a time. And don't be discouraged by continual rejections. Next to zucchini squash, poetry must be the most overproduced commodity in the world. You might ask yourself how much poetry you yourself read in current magazines; how many books of poetry you buy per year. If poetry were dependent upon people like you to survive, how well would it thrive? Are you sure you are submitting to the right sorts of places for the kind of poetry you write? Talk these matters over, along with your poetry and that of others, in your writing group. Study the magazines listed in *Poet's Market* and *Writer's Market* (published by Writer's Digest Books) and the *International Directory of Little Magazines and Small Presses* (published by Dustbooks), which lists many of the small literary magazines where poets can get a start. Order a sample copy of magazines you don't know but which sound interesting. And, of course, the more contemporary poetry you read and analyze, the better prepared you will be to write poetry that will be accepted.

It is when you begin thinking in terms of a book that the poetry market truly becomes depressing. After you have a number of "good" acceptances—that is, those in magazines respected in the literary world—you probably will begin thinking about a collection. Go to the library and study the volumes of poetry by individual poets (not anthologies). In the front of each there is usually a list of credits, indicating where the poems first appeared in magazines. Find a poet you respect and see where his or her poems have appeared. A page of credits will be of great importance to you in getting your first book accepted. Book publishers are not likely to consider seriously poets who have not established a fairly impressive record in the magazines.

When you have your collection (with its all-important credit page) typed up and organized in the form in which you want it to appear, you begin the difficult job of finding a publisher. Unless you have connections with one of the trade publishers—that is, the important, big houses, mostly in New York and Boston—it is a waste of time to send your book of poetry to them. It may have happened that such a publisher received a book by an unknown and brought it out, but I have never heard of such a case. You will have more luck with the small publishers listed in *Poet's Market* and *Writer's Market* or the *International Directory*. Study the descriptions of the publishers carefully, and inquire first, perhaps sending a small sample of your poetry. Some publishers will offer cooperative arrangements, by which you pay part of the cost of publication. That is a perfectly respectable practice—and not to be confused with the well-known ''subsidy publishers'' or ''vanity presses,'' the big companies which advertise widely that they will publish your work at your expense. These are called ''vanity'' operations because they customarily respond even to the poorest writing with fulsome praise, with maybe a touch of criticism here and there for credibility. Their prices are high, and—fairly or not—their label on a book is almost a guarantee that it will be ignored by reviewers, who receive dozens of such books (all mailed out at the author's expense) and usually bypass them without looking at them, so prevalent is their reputation for publishing work of poor quality.

You will do much better with a small and relatively unknown publisher, even if you have to pay part of the publication costs. Or you may want to consider self-publication, which is a time-honored recourse of many good (and more not-so-good) writers. You should understand the difference between a printer and a publisher. A printer prints—and manufactures books. A publisher is a broker who, at least theoretically, undertakes to market books, or make them available to the public. Some publishers have printing plants and do their own work, but many—even the big ones—also farm out work to printers. If you want to have your own work printed, go to a printer, not a publisher. It is much cheaper. You can put any name you can think of on the cover as publisher: Perma Press, or whatever. It is not the business of the printer to judge the quality of the work: he prints what you pay him to print (unless it is illegal). You can find advertisements for mail-order printers in magazines, or local printers in the yellow pages of your phone book. Even the small "quick-print" printers have facilities for producing relatively good-looking pamphlets—and that may be the simplest and least expensive way for you to get some of your work into print.

A publisher (not a subsidy publisher) pays for the printing and manufacture of the books—in exchange for exclusive control of your copyright. Like printers, publishers are in business for profit. But the publisher's business is more of a gamble. An editor makes a judgment on a manuscript: "I think we can sell enough copies of this book to pay the printing costs and make a profit." He then offers the author a royalty contract, often with an advance. The advance is a cash payment to be deducted from royalties. For example, the contract might offer you royalties of 10% and an advance of $500. That means you will get 10% of the list price of the books sold. Some contracts are based on net, rather than list, price. If the book lists at $10 per copy, you will start getting royalty checks after the first 500 are sold (covering the $500 which was advanced to you). Meanwhile, you have promised not only not to offer the same work to any other publisher, but also not to have it printed yourself. This means that the publisher has the sole right to print and distribute copies of your work.

All this makes sense in terms of prose books, which have a market. If a publisher has a hot item, it pays to advertise and promote the book, arrange personal appearances for the author, see to it that the book is widely reviewed and discussed. In fact, however, not even most books of prose are "hot items," and publishers bring out many more books each year than they actively advertise and promote. These are gambles—like buying mineral rights on farms in the hope that someday someone might find oil in the vicinity. Maizie Blaze is an unknown whose writing appears to have promise. Blowhard Press brings out a book of hers, sends out review copies, and waits. Nothing much happens. The printed books remain in the warehouse. Maizie writes a second book (and by contract has agreed to send it to Blowhard). It is printed, and still nothing happens, and those books, too, are in the warehouse. But for some reason her third book attracts attention. (Maybe she has meanwhile married the Sultan of Zuq and left him for a trapeze artist.) Once a book begins to sell, the publisher begins to promote it. And if there is now a lot of interest in Maizie, it is mighty convenient for the publisher to have the rights to those first two books tied up.

But you can imagine that such a story has almost no relevance to poetry. There is simply is no market to speak of. Even the books of the best-known poets are often published in editions of only a thousand or so, and fewer than that are ever sold. Advances, if any, are small, promotion is minimal, and neither the poet nor the publisher makes money. Books of poetry are considered by the publishers as "prestige" items, published for the same reason that an oil company or greeting-card company might sponsor a production of some major cultural event on television, not directly to sell oil or greeting cards, but to enhance the reputation of the company. How much prestige are they going to get out of publishing your work?

Because of these conditions, even the best poets are likely to start with the small presses, with self-publication, or with cooperative publishing arrangements. Sales of even a few hundred copies of a book of poetry are remarkable. Poets support themselves by other means. Their reputations as poets may lead to foundation grants or awards or promotions or reading engagements or other advantages, but they earn little by direct sales of their poetry. Most literary magazines pay only in contributor's copies, or nominal sums of a few dollars for a poem. (Rates of a dollar a line are excellent and rare—which adds up to $14 for a sonnet.) And rates in the magazines of general circulation are not much better. I was (in the 1960s) paid $10 per line for a twenty-line poem by *Ladies' Home Journal*. That was tops. And a very successful poet cannot expect to have more than, say, a dozen poems in national magazines a year. There just aren't many spots to fill, and editors will not take more than two or three poems from a given poet in a year.

The currency of a poetic career is not cash but reputation—and that, too, is a mixed bag in regard to its merits. At any given time in the

United States there are about two hundred "known" poets. (How many can you name?) These mostly know or know of one another. They show up on the committees to grant awards and prizes, give readings at colleges and elsewhere, appear regularly in the respectable literary journals (such as *Poetry, American Poetry Review,* or *New York Quarterly*). Often they not only give but get the grants. Though they represent a diversity of talents and tastes, they constitute the literary establishment—at least in regard to poetry. They are not to be confused with writers who make money on books—writers such as Norman Mailer, John Updike, Herman Wouk, Saul Bellow, or Erica Jong. (Of these, Updike and Jong are poets, but that is a sideline in regard to making money.) Getting into that circle of two hundred requires a lot more politics and pull and personality than it does poetic talent. Given the whimsicality of taste in our culture, there is no way of saying which poets are actually "best," or even which are likely to be read twenty years from now. (A list from twenty years ago would be almost totally obscure to us today.) I am not sure I would recommend to any poet that he or she play the game of trying to become one of the "known" poets under these circumstances. I played it for some twenty years, with some success, but I found it corrupting, and decided I had better things to do with my remaining years.

Such as write poetry. This is the point most difficult to explain, but the one I would most like to make to those who contemplate devoting a substantial portion of their lives to poetry. Like virtue, poetry is its own reward. Well, sure, we are likely to respond, but aren't there some other rewards, too? Some, indeed, may accrue, but you have little to do with it. Poetry has made some few famous, but none very rich, and the circumstances that create this kind of success are very much a matter of chance. Will the poetry that you write touch a public nerve as sensitively as T. S. Eliot did with his *The Waste Land,* as Allen Ginsberg did with his *"Howl"*? It depends on a lot more than your talent and efforts or the quality of your poetry. Even those two poems, which spoke to their times about as effectively as any poetry ever did—and brought their poets a considerable degree of recognition and material success—are not widely read (and, when read, not well understood) today, within their own century. Set your sights higher. Will you write a poem that will endure, as Milton's *Paradise Lost* or Goethe's *Faust* have endured? You will never know. Certainly, these poets could not know how their work would be received in later centuries. By whom? Scholars and critics? How many people do you know who have read *Paradise Lost* or *Faust*? Have you?

The immortality game, like that of getting into the circle of the two hundred, can be wicked and delusionary. If you were a physicist you might measure your success in terms of having solved some recognized problems in the material structure of the universe. If you were an engineer, you might measure it by having erected specific structures or managed forces that have some discernible effect in the world. And the models of careers we have available in our society are based on premises such as these. But there really is no "career" as a poet. You will never know whether you are successful in publicly recognized terms.

That leaves you with perhaps the most important reward of all: personal satisfaction. I was talking to a poet recently who said that, at this point in his life, he wrote only for himself. I pointed out to him that although he obviously was intelligent and talented and capable, his work (which he showed me—so I guess he wasn't writing *only* for himself) was careless in structure, needlessly obscure, marred by cheap flamboyance of language, and more intellectual than deeply felt. He acknowledged these faults but guessed that since he was writing primarily for his own satisfaction, he didn't worry much about them. He wasn't motivated to clean up his act because he wasn't going to take it out into the public arena.

That seems to me like eating nothing but potato chips because you are dining alone. Keep it up long enough and you'll suffer from malnutrition. I have no more exacting audience than myself. Since I have no expectations of any other reward from most of the poetry I write than the reward of personal satisfaction, I have no reason to write anything other than the very best I can. There's no hurry: I can work on a poem for years. No one is hammering at the door wanting my copy for the printer. I don't have to worry about what others may think, and so am not concerned about current fashions. My only concern is quality—as I perceive it—for that is the only thing about writing poetry which brings me satisfaction. Well, to be honest, I am not as pure as these sentences suggest—and I am at times lured by a desire to be widely read and recognized. But to the extent that I am so lured, my poetry suffers.

You are more likely to succeed in poetry, as in love, if you get success out of your head. Concentrate on quality. Learn the joy of creating excellence—whether or not anyone else recognizes it. You will soon find that your own standards are higher than those around you, anyway (that is, your standards for your own work; others might have higher standards for what they are trying to do).

I would guess you will find your life in poetry a stirring mixture of all these elements, sometimes requiring compromises. It certainly helps to have a circle of other writers with whom you exchange work and opinions. (Incidentally, especially if you are isolated, it helps to have a few pen pals with whom you can exchange poems and reactions. You can find beginning poets whose work you admire in the little literary magazines—and write them in care of the magazine to establish contact.) You will, of course, want to try your poems on magazines and eventually to think of the possibilities of book publication, but I hope this discussion will help you put that process into some perspective, to realize that, after all, the primary objective is the satisfaction you have yourself in practicing a difficult art, and that the question of your public acceptance as a poet is of secondary importance.

Versification Chart

Types of Meter

syllabic meter: line length determined by syllable count only.

quantitative meter: line length determined by number of feet, defined in terms of long and short syllables rather than of stressed and unstressed. Applies to Latin and Greek poetry, rarely to English.

accentual meter: line length determined by number of beats, or strong stresses, disregarding number of syllables and minor stresses.

accentual syllabic meter: line length determined by number of feet, in English defined by units of stressed and unstressed syllables.

Line Lengths
(with accent marks to assist pronunciation)

monómeter (a line of one foot)	**pentámeter** (five feet)
dímeter (two feet)	**hexámeter,** or **Alexandrine** (six feet)
trímeter (three feet)	**septámeter** (seven feet)
tetrámeter (four feet)	**octámeter** (eight feet)

Common Accentual Syllabic Feet
(units with stressed and unstressed syllables as indicated)

iamb, iambic—da DUM: an I \ amb IS \ a FOOT \ in VERSE \ that's CALLED \ i AM \ bic (Final unstressed syllable is **hypermetrical,** i.e., it doesn't count in the **scansion,** or analysis of the line into feet.)

trochee, trochaic—DUM da: TRO chees \ MARCH in \ MOURN ful \ NUM bers \

pyrrhic—da da: a PYR \ rhic FOOT \ is an \ er RAT \ ic ONE \ (third foot pyrrhic) (Two or more pyrrhics cannot be used in sequence. Many pyrrhics can take a slight stress on one of their syllables and so may be regarded as **theoretical** iambs or trochees. In the example above, *is an* can be read as a theoretical trochee, but not as an iamb.)

spondee, spondaic—DUM DUM: SEE THESE \ BRASS TACKS \ HOLD WHITE \ SHEETS FAST \ (Two or more spondees rarely occur in sequence. When they do, as in the example above, one of the two syllables is likely to take a slightly stronger stress, so the foot is read as a trochee [SEE these] or iamb [brass TACKS].)

anapest, anapestic—da da DUM: with a SKIP \ and a HOP \ will the AN \ a pest TROT \

dactyl, dactylic—DUM da da: GONE are the \ DAYS when the \ DAC tyl was\ POP u lar\

These six feet account for almost all accentual poetry in English. The norm is predominantly iambic verse with the other feet substituted for iambs as variations. (Dactyls almost never occur as variations in iambic or anapestic verse.) Some poems are, however, predominantly trochaic, anapestic, or dactylic. (Predominantly pyrrhic or spondaic verse is impossible.) In trochaic verse, pyrrhics, spondees, and dactyls work as occasional variations. In anapestic verse, iambs work as variations. Iambic and anapestic meters are called **rising rhythms.** Trochaic and dactylic meters are called **falling rhythms.** Another common variation in accentual syllabic meter is the **monosyllabic foot** (also called **truncated** or **catalectic foot**), a single stressed syllable (or an iamb, trochee, anapest, or dactyl without their unstressed syllable or syllables). Often pyrrhics and spondees are used in combination: da da DUM DUM or (less often) DUM DUM da da. This combination is called an **Ionic,** after a four-syllable foot in Greek metrics; an Ionic counts as two feet in English scansion. In addition to the above, the following may sometimes occur in English verse:

Rare Accentual Syllabic Feet

amphibrach—da DUM da: the SOUND of \ the HORNS in \ the MORN ing \

(Note that this could also be scanned: the SOUND \ of the HORNS \ in the MORN \ ing. When a line can be explained in terms of the six common feet given above, that is probably the best explanation, as poets writing in English generally compose in those feet. This line can best be read as an anapestic line, with an iamb as a variation in the first foot and a hypermetrical syllable at the end, though, alternatively, it can be thought of as three regular amphibrachs. Similarly, the rest of these "rare" feet can usually better be scanned in terms of the common feet above.

amphimacer—DUM da DUM: FACE the WILD \ WIND, and STAND \ STOUT ly NOW \

tribrach—da da da: and THAT \ was my LONG \ SCYTHE WHIS \ per ing to \ the GROUND \ (Fourth foot is a tribrach; see Chapter 6.)

molussus—DUM DUM DUM: i BLANCHED \ be FORE \ the MAN'S \ GREAT STONE FACE \ (fourth foot is a molussus.)

bacchius—da DUM DUM: when DAY BREAKS \ the FISH BITE \ at SMALL FLIES \

antibacchius—DUM DUM da: BLIND LUCK is \ LOVED MORE than \ HARD THINK ing \

Length of Units
(verse paragraphs, stanzas, or strophes)

monostich: one-line unit (or one-line poem)   **cinquain:** five lines
couplet, or **distich:** two lines   **sestet:** six lines
triplet, or **tercet:** three lines   **septet:** seven lines
quatrain: four lines   **octave:** eight lines
  (Longer units are simply called by number: a nine-line stanza, ten-line strophe, etc.)

Common Sonnet Forms

(usually iambic pentameter poems of fourteen lines with these rhyme schemes)

	Italian (or **Petrarchan**)	English (or **Shakespearean**)	Spenserian
octave	a	a	a
	b	b	b *quatrain*
	b	a	a
	a	b	b
	a	c	b
	b	d	c *quatrain*
	b	c	b
	a	d	c
sestet	c c c c	e	c
	d d d d *tercet*	f	d *quatrain*
	e c c c	e	c
	c d d e	f *sestet*	d
	d c d d *tercet*	g	e *couplet*
	e d c c	g	e

Index to Terms

Index to Poets Quoted

Index to Works of Poetry Quoted

Printed in the United States
70676LV00002B/239